Ships, Strikes and Keelmen

David Bell

ISBN: 1 901237 26 5

Printed and published by TUPS Books,
30 Lime Street, Newcastle upon Tyne, NE1 2PQ
Tel: 0191 2330990 Fax: 0191 2330578

Foreword

History is a continuous spectrum, but often bright glimpses, like flashes of lightning across a dark turbulent sky, briefly illuminate the whole and help us to make sense of it.

Or so I hope, for that is the purpose of this book.

During the nineteenth century, the North-East of England was possibly the most important industrial area in the world, and the skill and ingenuity of our forefathers helped to make Britain great.

None of us should ever forget that and their truly heroic efforts should be remembered with pride.

Acknowledgements

I would like to thank the following local historians and friends who have given me every assistance in my studies and research;

Jim Cuthbert, Robert F. Wray, Alan Turner, Capt S. Butterworth, Janice Blower, Alton Pickersgill, Kathleen Tate, Mrs H. Whale, K. Bardwell, Shauna Gregg and Staff at South Tyneside Central Library.

Also I would like to thank *The Shields Gazette* for their co-operation and the use of photographic material and quotations from past issues of their excellent newspaper, the oldest local newspaper in the country.

Contents

Chapter 1	The Tyneside Keelmen and the Great Strike of 1819	Page 1
2	Palmers' Shipyard and the Old 'John Bowes'	Page 9
3	Garibaldi on Tyneside	Page 15
4	The Roots of the Tyneside Music Hall	Page 31
5	When The 'Makems' Showed the Way	Page 49
6	Palmers' Warships	Page 61
7	The First to Sink a 'Sub.'!	Page 85
8	The Death of the 'Olympic'	Page 91
	Epilogue	Page 105
	Final Word	Page 106
	Bibliography	Page 107

The Tyneside Keelmen and the Great Strike of 1819

Keel passing Felling Shore
(an engraving by W.J Palmer)

In the early nineteenth century the management of the River Tyne was still the jealously-guarded privilege of the Newcastle City Corporation. Far from having the foresight to see that the City, and indeed all of Tyneside, would benefit if the depth and width of the river were properly maintained, the Corporation allowed vessels to dump solid ballast into the river in return for the payment of

A dreaded sight; keelmen gathering for a 'spree'

dues. So, in order to protect their own income, the City Corporation allowed the river to fall into such a poor condition that larger vessels could not use it at all, and even quite small vessels could not get alongside Newcastle Quay or the coal-loading chutes for fear of grounding.

Almost the only cargo which was exported from the Tyne in those early days of the industrial revolution was coal and, in order to transport it to the ocean-going vessels which lay at the mouth of the river, small, flat-bottomed craft known as 'keels' were employed. These vessels, which could carry eight chauldrons (about 20 tons) in their single hold, were wind and punt driven. The word 'keel' is very ancient and is thought to have originated from the Anglo-Saxon word for the ships, *ceols*, which brought the invaders to these isles.

The keels were filled from loading chutes known as 'spouts', which were fed by wagonways leading down to the shore at such places as Dunston, Blaydon and Walker. Then, fully-laden, they were navigated through the treacherous shallows by the keelmen.

To serve the larger vessels, which lay at the mouth of the Tyne, the keelmen had to navigate several

'The Plundering of All Hallows' from a print by R. Waters.

miles of river. This job was fraught with perils, as may be deduced from contemporary songs and also from the visible evidence of wrecks which still litter the river-bed, despite more than a century's passage of time. Visible proof of this can be seen in the outline of the wreck which can be seen off Brett's Oils, near the Metro Bridge, at low tide.

The men who manned these vessels were sturdy and independent. As local historian Eric Forster says,"they were the very stuff of folklore".

The crew of a keel was made up of two or three men and a boy who, for some now unknown reason, was called the 'peedee'.

The 'keel bullies', as they were fond of calling themselves, were a hard-drinking and violent lot and it is well known that keelmen, especially when 'on the spree', were beyond reason. Tyneside historian Johnson adds that the keelman's "ignorance was amazing and was only redeemed by his rough native humour".

Though the butt of many jokes and the frequent target of satirical writers, the keelmen were feared by all. The local authorities had very little control

The Keelmen's Hospital, as it appears today

over them, especially as they stuck together, protecting their own kind from arrest or punishment.

Typical of their lawlessness was their looting of the ruins of All Hallows Church during its demolition in 1786. We learn from contemporary sources that "drunken persons and keelmen.......made off with much timber". Furthermore, though these acts were witnessed by spectators and officials, no action could be taken against the culprits, who escaped by way of the river.

The very fact that the keelmen stuck together was something of a virtue, however. Many years before any official form of welfare state had been established, the rough, drunken keelmen of the Tyne had set up institutions to look after their own kind.

The Keelmen's Hospital, which still stands today, was built in 1701 to house those keelmen who were too old or infirm to earn their own living. The Hospital was built entirely from funds raised among the keelmen themselves, each boat paying a levy for the erection, maintenance and running costs of the building.

The keelmen also funded and built their own church in their own area of the town, just outside the Sandgate, where they could attend services away from the critical eye of the 'good citizens' of the town. This church, St Ann's, was built in 1768 and is still in use today, though there are no longer any 'keel bullies' or their families amongst the congregation.

The *Newcastle Courant* of 2nd October, 1819, reported "we regret to state that the keelmen upon the Tyne have held meetings and, generally, have struck working." That this was not an unique occurrence may be judged by the fact that the information is given on the back page of the newspaper and in the same column are such items as the announcement that Sir Thomas Burdon had decided to increase his hospital subscription to five guineas annually. Nevertheless this strike, though lasting less than a month, was to be possibly the most eventful of the strikes of the Tyneside keelmen.

Keelmen's strikes of sufficient note to have been recorded had occurred in 1654, 1671, 1709, 1710, 1740, 1750, 1771, 1794 and 1805. The latter three, however, had the same cause as the strike of 1819 — the construction of staithes by the coalowners. As the

One of the hated staithes which the keelmen attacked by night

keelmen had complained to the Corporation at the time of the 1771 strike, these staithes were for the sole purpose of "saving keel dues". Staithes carried the coal spouts out into the middle of the river, so that the bigger, deeper-draughted vessels could be loaded without the use of keels.

As the *Newcastle Courant* reported at the start of the 1819 strike, the keelmen's complaint was "against the extension of the colliery spouts......below Newcastle bridge, by which vessels of almost any burthen can now receive their coals without the intervention of keels, thus throwing many keelmen out of employment".

One solution proposed by the keelmen, and reported in the *Courant*, was that the spouts should "pay a small tax to their hospital fund which, owing to the decrease of their employment, is greatly exhausted."

The other cause of the strike given in the *Courant* was that "the coalowners load more coals on board the keels than formerly; i.e that they keep up the nominal price by giving larger measure to the shipper, and thus increase the labour of the keelmen without any additional pay". The only other local newspaper of the time, the *Newcastle Weekly Chronicle*, adds nothing to these complaints but states that "during the first three days of this week, not fewer than 400 sail arrived in the Tyne. Long continued winds from the northeast had detained them, and now the keelmen detain them here".

From this last piece of information, it seems reasonable to deduce that the strike was having positive results. Indeed, inspection of the 'shipping intelligence' column of the *Courant* reveals that no foreign-going vessel whatsoever had managed to sail from the Tyne that week, against a normal weekly total of a dozen or more. By the following week, though there were no further reports in either paper about the strike, even the number of coastwise vessels cleared from the Tyne was down to less than half the normal total.

It was against this worrying background that, in the words of both the *Courant* and the *Chronicle* (they carried identical reports), "the mayor of this

A Tyneside Volunteer

town had proceeded down the river with the civil power, aided by the boats of His Majesty's ships, with a view of opening the navigation of the river (which had been interrupted for the last fortnight by the riotous proceedings of the keelmen) and had gone on shore at North Shields".

The keelmen resisted his authority with showers of sticks, stones and abuse. A detachment of the 6th Dragoons was called to restore order and they fired upon the crowd, killing one man, Joseph Cleckson, and wounding several.

One of the keelmen who had been apprehended during the melee was then rescued by his mates, who broke down the doors of the *Northumberland Arms* and attacked the mayor's constables in order to free him. The mayor barely escaped with his life through the back door. According to the *Chronicle*, the infuriated keelmen threatened to "burn His Majesty's men of war" if the dragoon who "fired the fatal shot" was not handed over to them to punish as they saw fit.

The *Chronicle* of the 16th October also reported that the keelmen "have this week threatened to pull down some of the staithes" and, indeed, on the night before the North Shields riot, three keelmen had carried out an unsuccessful attack on the staith at Wallsend. The *Chronicle* of the 23rd October reported that the three keelmen were known by name and had been fined £15 each by the County Court in their absence, they having absconded or were being harboured by their friends.

The authorities further responded with a claim, reported in the *Chronicle*, that a large warship was imminently expected in the Tyne with 300 marines aboard. Things had indeed taken a serious turn.

At this juncture, both sides apparently decided that "enough was enough". The morning after the North Shields riot, the keelmen returned to work. The *Newcastle Courant* reported that "we have much pleasure in informing the public that the

Keelbully
(from the author's own sketchpad)

North Shields in the Age of Steam; an engraving by W. J. Palmer

misunderstanding between the keelmen and their employers has been happily terminated". Once it had been made clear to the keelmen that nothing "was extorted from them", the coalowners were pleased "to relieve the present wants and provide for the future support of an industrious body of men".

The *Chronicle* also reported that the settlement provided for an increase in the coalowners' contributions towards the keelman's hospital from £1800 to £2700 per annum.

Both sides had apparently withdrawn with honour, but in the long run the keelmen's cause was hopeless. The needs of an industrialised nation could not be served by such an antiquated system of transporting the coal needed to power the 'age of steam' which was to follow.

It was significant that a further concession offered in the strike settlement was that "the Corporation have determined to employ those keelmen who may want work in improving the navigation of the river".

In other words, they were being offered the opportunity to dig their own graves.

Palmers' Shipyard and the Old 'John Bowes'

'Charlie' Palmer in his youthful prime, a true 'Captain of Industry'

Even in the prosaic world of industry, fate can play such a powerful hand in human affairs that it stretches the credulity of coincidence. Such a case is the astonishing link between the working life of the ship *John Bowes* and the Jarrow shipyard which built her.

Up until mid-Victorian times, the commercial life of Tyneside was completely dependent upon the fortunes of the coal trade with London. A huge fleet of collier brigs, sailing vessels of usually 200 tons or less in burden, shipped the 'sea coal' to the capital.

By the 1840's, however, the increasing competition of railborne coal from the Yorkshire and Midland coalfields was calling into question the speed and efficiency of the Tyneside coal trade.

It was a rich irony that the prosperity of the North East of England was being threatened by the success of its greatest contribution to industrialisation — steam-powered railways.

Charles Mark Palmer, a young entrepreneur with amazing courage of his convictions, saw clearly what must be done. In 1851, he and his brother purchased a small shipyard at Jarrow and began to build steam-powered iron ships. The first such vessel they built, *Northumberland*, was a tug, but the very next vessel, *John Bowes*, was to revolutionise the coal-carrying trade and safeguard Tyneside's continued prosperity.

The keel of the *John Bowes* was laid in the very first year that Palmers' Yard began operations and she was launched on Wednesday the 30th June, 1852. She was not the first iron ship to be built, nor even the first steam-powered single-screw vessel. But she *was* the first to combine these features and prove their commercial viability in a cargo-carrying vessel.

The 'John Bowes' after her major refit of 1883

Palmers' Integrated Works, from the River, engraved by W. J. Palmer

Two previous vessels of similar construction, *Bedlington* (1841) and *QED* (1844), had proven financial disasters, both running aground and breaking up before the owners had even recouped their outlay.

John Bowes' twin-cylinder simple expansion engine, built by Robert Stephenson of Newcastle, developed 70 nominal horse-power and produced a service speed of 6 to 7 knots, with a top speed of 9 knots. This was without the assistance of the full sailing-ship rig which she carried on her three masts, shown in the photo opposite. To ensure a fast turnaround in port, other distinctive features were incorporated in her design. These were her unusually long single hatchway (60ft) and the fitting of double-bottom tanks for the carriage of water on the return trip rather than the more usual solid ballast.

The enormous cost of this unique vessel, £10,000, almost three times the cost of the average collier brig, must have been a tremendous gamble for Palmer, but his faith was amply justified, and his fortune assured, by her very first voyage.

Loading 650 tons of coal at Sunderland in 4 hours, she sailed on the 28th July, 1852, and completed her maiden voyage, to Blackwall in the Thames, within 48 hours. Taking 24 hours to discharge and

48 hours for the return trip, she completed in 5 days a voyage which the average collier brig, with fair winds and carrying less than half the payload, would have taken a month to complete!

In her first year of life, the *John Bowes* proved her consistency, completing 17 such voyages and carrying a total of 9,483 tons of coal to the Thames.

This was tremendous publicity for Palmers' Yard and full vindication of the brothers' business acumen. During the next 18 months, ten such vessels were built by the Jarrow yard and other shipyards on Tyneside were quick to follow the example. By the end of 1855, 36 iron-screw colliers were operating out of the Tyne, bringing great prosperity and commercial success to the river.

Palmers' Yard grew into the only industrial complex in the world which could, quite literally, take in raw iron ore at one end of the works and turn out a complete ship at the other.

Meanwhile, the vessel which had made all this possible continued to ply her trade, growing increasingly more grimy and disreputable in appearance as she voyaged back and forth from the river.

Although he sold the vessel to B.G Barnett in 1873, Palmer never forgot his debt to the *John Bowes*. In a banquet speech as late as 1886, when it must have seemed that the old ship was nearing the end of her useful working life, Palmer was to state "I do not know any event in my long and eventful career that has given me greater pleasure than the success which has attended the introduction of that steamer".

The common folk of Tyneside, more than 7000 of whom were employed by Palmers' Works at that time, certainly agreed with him. A street ballad of the time rejoiced in the old *John Bowes*, "what gans stottin' alang by hersell".

Amazingly, despite hardships and setbacks, neither the *John Bowes* nor the yard which had built her ever ceased trading throughout the twenty years of the Great Depression, which lasted from the mid-1870's until the mid-1890's. In fact, Palmers' Yard actually broke production records twice in the 1880's and Barnett Brothers re-engined the *John Bowes* in 1883, fitting a more modern two-cylinder compound engine and boiler.

In 1895, writing his definitive work 'The Making of the River Tyne', R.W. Johnson suggested that, at the end of her working life, the *John Bowes* should be given "a last honourable resting place among the wooden walls of England, lying snugly in Portsmouth harbour".

Alas, it was not to be! There is little sentiment in business and, in the following year, 1896, the old ship was sold by Barnetts to Mr McKenzie of Dublin, who intended her for the Limerick trade. She graced the lovely waters of the Shannon for less than a year, however, before being sold on to C.H. Pile, shipbrokers, of London.

In 1898, the brokers sold her to Norwegian

owners, who renamed her *Spec*, and she never again carried the Red Ensign. In 1900, she was given the rather more dignified name *Transit* when she passed to Swedish owners and then, in 1908, she became *Carolina* when she was taken under the Spanish flag. Later, still under Spanish ownership, she became the *Valentin Fierro* and finally, in 1932, the *Villa Selgas*. Even under foreign ownership, however, she continued to visit the Tyne, and the photograph overleaf shows her passing Palmers in 1906.

Meanwhile, throughout the old ship's changes of name and fortune, Palmers' Yard continued to build ships, more than a thousand of them. But the shipyard too was suffering declining fortunes and in 1932, when the *John Bowes* took on her last identity, Palmers' Yard built its last ship. This vessel was *HMS Duchess*, which was completed in July 1932. No more ships were to roll off the stocks at Palmers, and no more names were to be given to the old *John Bowes*.

On Saturday the 14th October, 1933, in a gale off Ribadesella, en route from Bilbao to San Estaban de Pravia, the *Villa Selgas*, ex-*John Bowes*, sprang a leak. She was carrying a cargo of iron ore, so there was no possibility of saving her, and the crew abandoned her to sink. No lives were lost and, as the *Shields Gazette* pointed out, it was a dignified end for the old steamer and "some consolation to know that she was of service to the last, and did not come to an inglorious end on the scrap heap".

Not so the yard which had built her, which stood empty and deserted for another year, before being bought by National Shipbuilders Security Ltd, who allowed the site to be plundered for scrap and levelled.

Thus, the useful life of the shipyard and the most famous vessel it produced were virtually co-incidental. It was as though one could not exist without the other.

John Bowes, Durham pitowner after whom the revolutionary vessel was named

'Transit' (ex 'John Bowes') passes her birthplace over 50 years after her launch

Garibaldi on Tyneside

The entrance to the Tyne, engraved by W. J. Palmer

On Tuesday the 21st of March, 1854, the people of Tyneside awoke to the exciting news that the ship of Giuseppe Garibaldi, Lion of Italy and late Defender of the Roman Republic (see biographical notes to follow), was in the river!

As Master of the sailing vessel *Commonwealth*, he had brought his ship safely across the bar at 7.30 a.m on the early morning tide and was lying at anchor off North Shields, lightening ship into the ballast keels. The *Commonwealth*, a large vessel of 1000 tons burden, was too deep to lay alongside her intended berth at South Shields, where she was to take on a full cargo of coal for Genoa.

Of much greater importance than her cargo, however, was Garibaldi's secret intention to place the fast and well-found vessel under the command of the forces of the *Risorgimento* and the cause of

One of the new coal-staithes which had virtually put the keelmen out of business

Italian freedom as soon as she reached Italian waters.

To this end, though arriving from Baltimore and flying the American flag, the vessel was partially manned by Italian *emigres*, many of very good family, intent upon offering their services to whomsoever would lead them in uniting Italy and freeing her forever from foreign domination. Her Italian owners were fully aware of Garibaldi's intentions, the cargo being to some extent a 'blind' so that the fast clipper could slip past her enemies unmolested, in the guise of a merchant ship.

Notwithstanding the motley nature of his crew, Garibaldi was no amateur sailor, his early life having been spent at sea. All reports maintain that, whether or not the voyage was a 'blind', he was a hard taskmaster and handled his vessel, crew and cargo in a fully professional manner. No man was more worthy of the respect of Tyneside's Master Mariners.

When she was light enough to lie alongside her berth without grounding, the *Commonwealth* was brought to the staithes of the Pontop and Shields Railway Company.

There she discharged the remainder of her solid ballast on to the growing heap behind the northeast

'King Bomba' shows Pope 'Pio Nono' how to bombard his own subjects

end of South Shields market place, a site which later became Brigham's Dock and is now part of the Market Dock housing development.

When deballasting was complete, the *Commonwealth* began taking on her cargo from railway wagons via the staithes.

Meanwhile, the word was spreading like wildfire on Tyneside, where no leader was more universally popular and respected than Garibaldi among the working people.The cause of Italian liberation, and especially the part Garibaldi had played in the struggle, had fired the imagination of the British public. In working-class industrial areas such as Tyneside, this feeling was particularly strong and there were loud and insistent calls for armed intervention to help the insurgents.

Most fair-minded and decent people were incensed at the cruelties perpetrated by the Austrians who ruled Northern Italy and such tyrants as '*King Bomba*' (Ferdinand II, King of the Two Sicilies), who earned his nickname by slaughtering whole cities by cannon-fire.

Indeed, when their government failed to respond, the British public were not above taking the law into their own hands, as on the occasion of the

The Duchess of Sutherland's reception (from The Illustrated London News)

Austrian General Haynau's visit to Barclay's Brewery, when the draymen set upon his party and beat them all up, to the horror and embarrassment of the British government.

Whatever the government's public stance, however, many of its members agreed with Lord Palmerston, who, although disapproving of the draymen's violent actions, wrote; "they should have tossed him in a blanket, rolled him in the kennel, and sent him home".

Other British citizens, such as Joseph Cowen, as mentioned elsewhere in this book, constantly agitated on behalf of the Italian Patriots. Some, such as Sidney Milnes Hawkes, later landlord of the Marsden Grotto Inn, and Colonel Hugh Forbes, a hero of Garibaldi's retreat from Rome, actually went out to Italy to fight.

If, in the cause of secrecy, Garibaldi had hoped to slip by unnoticed on his visit to South Shields, he was to be disappointed indeed! While the great man was tending his ship and hoping to rapidly and inconspicuously load the cargo which was to serve as his 'alibi', an official message arrived from the dignitaries of Newcastle, offering him a civic reception and banquet.

Garibaldi, whom the *Newcastle Courant* declared to be "of retired habits" politely and firmly "declined any public demonstration on his behalf" for, as the *Monthly Chronicle* further explained to its readers, "like all heroes, he was as modest as he was brave".

And indeed there was some truth in this assertion, because, besides the obvious need to avoid alerting his enemies by publicising his presence, Garibaldi *was* essentially a plain man. His early years at sea had bred into him a brusque impatience with formality and excessive ceremony of any kind.

A tale is told of him which amply demonstrates his hatred of snobbery. Before his arrival on Tyneside, when staying in London as the guest of the Duchess of Sutherland, he was so confused and harassed at the dinner table by the ministrations of a pompous servant that he leapt up and was only with great difficulty dissuaded from kicking the poor man's backside!

Notwithstanding Garibaldi's reluctance, however, the people of Tyneside were NOT prepared to allow him to depart without bestowing upon him some mark of their esteem and affection. At a meeting of the 'Friends of European Freedom' held at the Lecture Rooms, Newcastle, on the evening of Tuesday, March 28th 1854, it was resolved that a subscription list be opened to present the great man with a suitable memento of his visit to the Tyne.

When it was made public, the proposal was met with great enthusiasm in all quarters, and subscriptions flowed in from all parts of Tyneside. By far the greater part of the contributions were penny subscriptions from working men. An order was placed with Mr Joseph English, of Grey Street, Newcastle for a suitably inscribed sword and telescope, and the finished articles were handsome indeed. Both were engraved as follows:

> "Presented to General Garibaldi by the people of Tyneside, friends of European Freedom. April 1854"

The General had wished for no fuss or ceremony, but to turn down the gift of the common working people, to throw back their pennies in their faces, THAT was a different matter!

Garibaldi announced that he would accept their gift with pride, but the presentation had to take place quietly aboard his own vessel. Ominously, in spite of Garibaldi's wishes, the *Shields Gazette* reported that "the Liberals of Newcastle and Shields are preparing addresses".

In the event, what may have saved the great man from embarrassment was the very size of his

Keel of the Old Tyne, but the keelmen were fast disappearing by Garibaldi's day.

vessel. Too large to complete loading in the limited depths alongside the staithes, she had moved out to anchor in the river, to 'top off' from keelboats before the presentation was ready.

Although dredging and general river improvements had been taken in hand by the newly established Tyne Improvement Commission (constituted by Act of Parliament on the 15th July, 1850), approximately one-eighth of coal exports from the Tyne were still loaded from keels. It may well be imagined that Garibaldi, who no doubt shared the general Italian love of flamboyance and freedom of expression, would have got on very well with the keelmen, that dying breed of 'rough diamonds'!

The presentation party, which rowed out to the *Commonwealth* on the afternoon of the 11th April, was led by Mr Joseph Cowen, jnr., of Newcastle, and numbered less than 20 members, some of whom were mining delegates from the pitmen of the river. After reading quite a lengthy formal address, submitted by the 'Friends of European Freedom' and the Tyneside Liberals, which no doubt tried Garibaldi's patience sorely, Mr Cowen added the following simple words as he handed over the sword and telescope:

> "General,
>
> Along with this address I have to ask you to receive this sword and telescope. The intrinsic value of these articles is but small, and to a Republican chieftain who is accustomed to animate his compatriots by deeds of personal prowess, such a sword may be more ornamental than useful. But when I tell you that it is

Joseph Cowen Jnr, who campaigned ceaselessly in the cause of European liberty.

A Neapolitan soldier attempting to extinguish the fires of insurrection lit by Garibaldi (a cartoon from 'Don Pirlone', 1849)

purchased by the pennies of some hundreds of working men, contributed not only voluntarily but with enthusiasm, and that each penny represents a heart that beats true to European freedom, it will not, I think, be unworthy of your acceptance and preservation. We are not versed in the polite phraseology of diplomacy; of the refined conventionalism of courts we are ignorant. Representatives of the people, we have no costly presents to offer for your acceptance; but with that simplicity which best befits Republicans, we ask you to receive as a token of our esteem the articles before us."

The years were to prove Cowen wrong about the practical value of the sword. There is no doubt that Garibaldi regarded his 'English sword', as he called it, as a practical weapon. Indeed, he used it at the Battle of Volturno, on the 1st October, 1860, when he personally led the charge against the Bourbon regular troops.

He arrived at the battlefront in a carriage and, after both his driver and an accompanying officer were mortally wounded, "Garibaldi jumped out, sword in hand.....charged down the road at the astonished Neapolitans and sent them scampering back down the lane."

Garibaldi always preferred hand-to-hand combat and was particularly fierce in the use of the sword. During the siege of Rome, his sword became so bent and buckled with continuous heavy use that, when the fighting was over, it would no longer fit in its scabbard. His 'English sword', therefore, could have been no toy if it stood up to the use to which Garibaldi habitually put his weapons.

Perhaps mindful of his grandfather's wishes (see later in the letter Garibaldi sent to Cowen as he left the Tyne), Garibaldi's grandson, General Giuseppe Garibaldi (1879-1950) brought the sword with him when he volunteered to fight for the British in the Boer War, a conflict in which he served with great distinction.

He later carried the sword whilst fighting for the allies in World War One, volunteering to fight and raising an 'Italian Legion' of 14,000 men before Italy officially entered the War.

As far as I know, the sword is still with the Garibaldi family.

Garibaldi was very moved on receiving the sword and telescope,

Garibaldi with his 'English sword' c1860

which he turned in his hands and inspected minutely before replying:

> "Gentlemen, I am very weak in the English language, and can but imperfectly express my acknowledgements for your over great kindness. You honour me beyond my deserts. My services are not worthy of all the favour you have shown me. You more than reward me for any sacrifices I may have made in the cause of freedom.
>
> "One of the people, a workman like yourselves, I value very highly these expressions of your esteem, the more so because you testify thereby your sympathy for my poor, oppressed and down-trodden country. Speaking in a strange tongue, I feel most painfully my inability to thank you in terms sufficiently warm.
>
> "The future will alone show how soon it will be before I am called on to unsheath the noble gift I have just received and again battle in behalf of that which lies nearest my heart, the freedom of my native land. But be sure of this; Italy WILL one day be a nation, and its free citizens will know how to acknowledge all the kindness shown her exiled sons in the days of their darkest troubles.
>
> "Gentlemen, I would say more, but my bad English prevents me. You can appreciate my feelings and understand my hesitation. Again I thank you from my heart of hearts, and be confident of this, that whatever vicissitudes of fortune I may hereafter pass through, this sword shall never be drawn by me except in the cause of liberty."

The presentation being over, Mr Cowen proposed a toast to "General Garibaldi, and may the next time he visits the Tyne be as the citizen of an united Italian Republic". In which beverage this toast was pledged, we have no information, but it again moved Garibaldi profoundly, such that he turned dramatically to Cowen and said:

> "Should England at any time in a just cause need my arm, I am ready to unsheath in her defence this noble and splendid sword received at your hands".

Garibaldi then conducted the delegation on a tour of his vessel, displaying a lively interest in his visitors and questioning them about their occupations.

Discovering that one of his guests, Soloman Sutherland, was the President of the Working Men's Club and Institute of South Shields, which was the first such organisation to be founded in Britain, he questioned him closely as to the rules and objectives of the association.

His questions were so pertinent that Mr Sutherland formed the impression that, had he been able, Garibaldi would have applied for membership! In any event, the great man expressed his unreserved approval of the Institute and his good wishes for its future success.

One detail which did NOT meet with Garibaldi's approval, however, was the fact that the miners' delegation, as was the habit of their profession, were wearing hobnail boots.

Sailors in those days went barefoot or wore rope sandals to avoid damaging the holystoned wooden decks, which were the pride and joy of any ship's captain worth his salt. An apocryphal tale has it that, as they left the vessel, Garibaldi was heard to mutter;

"thank God they did not dance a hornpipe".

As their boat passed under the stern of his ship, all blissfully unaware of the great man's feelings, the delegation gave three hearty cheers for Garibaldi and the good ship *Commonwealth*.

Garibaldi sailed the following morning and, though he never returned to Tyneside, he was never forgotten, as can be seen by the list of 'mementos' of his visit to follow.

After the ship had sailed, a letter was delivered to Cowen, part of which is reproduced below.

Ship *Commonwealth*,
April 12th, 1854.

My Dear Cowen,
The generous manifestation of sympathy with which I have been honoured by you and your fellow citizens is of itself more than sufficient to recompense a life of the greatest merit........if ever England, your native country, should be so circumstanced as to require the help of an ally, cursed be that Italian who would not step forward with me in her defence......Farewell, my dear friend, but not adieu! Make room for me in your heart. Yours always and everywhere,
G Garibaldi

One suspects that the General had some help with his English in composing his speeches and this letter (after all, some members of his 'crew' represented the noblest and best-educated families of Italy), but the sentiments expressed are obviously sincere.

A painting of his ship *Commonwealth*, by the famous local marine artist John Scott, was later sent to Garibaldi, who treasured it all his life. He had it placed at the foot of his bed so that, each morning when he awoke, it was the first thing which met his eyes. It reminded him of some of the happiest hours of his turbulent life, a time of which he later wrote;

" what could be better than....traversing the ocean, hardened by a rough sailor's life in a struggle with the elements and danger....unapproachable and independent...."

Perhaps the painting also reminded him of the people of Tyneside, and of the friends he had made in the port of South Shields.

Brief Notes on the Life of Garibaldi

Giuseppe Garibaldi was born on the 4th July, 1807, at Nice, in the Kingdom of Piedmont/ Sardinia, which at the time was being occupied by the armies of Napoleon the Great.

Both his father and his grandfather had been seamen, and, when he was fifteen, Giuseppe followed them to sea. In February 1832, he qualified officially as a Master Mariner and, by the time he was twenty-five, had command of his own ship. But the times in which the young sea-captain lived were not conducive to a quiet and peaceful life at sea. Italy at the time was a patchwork of small States, ruled by foreigners and despots. Injustice and oppression were rife and the people were desperately poor. Many 'secret societies' were formed by patriots, determined to free their countrymen of oppression and to unite Italy into a single, fair and just State. It was not long before the honest, brave and impressionable Garibaldi was drawn into such intrigues and, in 1834, as a result of his part in a failed *coup*, he was exiled for the first time from his native land.

Garibaldi went to South America where he joined the insurgent forces fighting for freedom against the Brazilian Empire. Here, in the *pampas* around the River Plate, he learned his trade as a *Guerrilla* and rose to the command of the Italian Brigade, who wore the famous red shirts and thenceforth became known as the *Garibaldini*.

An original 'red shirt', Montevideo 1846

'Pio Nono' blesses the French troops after they had restored his temporal power
(an engraving from 'L'expedition de Rome', Paris 1851)

When, in 1848, the spontaneous uprisings in several of the oppressed States of Italy drew Garibaldi back to his homeland, he soon found employment as a leader of the patriot forces. Rome had declared herself independent of the despotic rule of the Pope, Pius IX (*Pio Nono*) and the Pontiff had called in the French to help him regain the city. Garibaldi's heroic, though unsuccessful, defence of the city against one of the major military forces of Europe made him a legend, especially amongst the working classes of Britain.

The inevitable end to the adventure, however, was another period of exile, and Garibaldi returned to his trade as a sea-captain, making voyages to as far away as China, while he brooded on the wrongs of his poor oppressed country.

Never willing to give up, he was back in Europe in 1854, as related within the pages of this book, to begin the series of great triumphs which led to the final victory, when Italy became united and free.

In 1864, after his conquests had led to the birth of

Garibaldi's tumultuous welcome in London
(from The London Illustrated News)

the Italian nation, Garibaldi returned to England "to pay a debt of gratitude" to the British people. His reception in London led to scenes without precedent. Half a million people turned out to witness the procession, in which representatives of trade unions and working men's committees proudly marched.

According to the *Times* correspondent, there had never been scenes quite like these in London before, and it was "most emphatically a people's welcome, a working-men's reception from first to last".

Incensed with jealousy, Karl Marx declared the parade to be "a miserable spectacle of imbecility".

Despite his mother's disapproval, the Prince of Wales entertained Garibaldi and Palmerston,

Gladstone and Lord John Russell invited him to dine with them. Queen Victoria was placed in a most awkward position by Garibaldi's tremendous popularity with the British public. After all, he had been an insurgent against the legitimate governments of friendly powers. Queen Victoria was so horrified by his enthusiastic reception in Britain that she expressed herself "half ashamed of a nation capable of such follies".

When she heard that her son had entertained Garibaldi at his official residence of Stafford House, she declared herself "very much shocked". In admonition, she wrote to Lord Russell;

> "The Queen much regrets the extravagant excitement respecting Garibaldi which shows little dignity and discrimination in the nation......The Queen fears that the Government may find Garibaldi's views and connections no little cause of inconvenience with foreign governments hereafter.......Brave and honest though he is, he has ever been a revolutionist leader."

In this last sentence, at least, she was right.

His life's work being done, Garibaldi then retired to the remote island of Caprera, where he farmed the stony soil and finally died on the 2nd of June, 1882.

It is a wonderful story, and I commend it to all readers.

Garibaldi on Caprera in old age.
He had taken to wearing his red shirt again

Mementos of Garibaldi's visit in the North East

In South Shields

Some thirty years after the General's visit, the dignitaries of South Shields commemorated the occasion by naming *Garibaldi Terrace*, at the foot of **Ocean Road.** The original name plaque, with an embossed image of the great man's head, can still be seen on house number 111.

The ordinary folk of South Shields, however, also remembered the visit and celebrated it in their own inimitable way by the formation of the **Garibaldi Brass Band** which, during its heydey at the turn of the century, met at George Dennett's stables in Claypath Lane. No doubt Mr Dennett had the most musical horses in town!

In Newcastle

In the City of Newcastle, at the corner of Nelson Street outside the Grainger Market, there is a plaque on the wall celebrating the visit of the General to a bookshop which once stood there.

In Sunderland

In the Pottery Gallery of **Sunderland Museum** there is a wonderful thrown-earthenware bowl, marked 'Dixon and Co.' which, besides some seemingly irrelevant inscriptions, shows a fine portrait of Garibaldi. The piece is dated c1860, at which time the great man had just embarked with his thousand volunteers on the conquest of Sicily.

His visit to Tyneside was probably very fresh in the minds of the general public at that time and no doubt the news of his latest adventure was greeted with great excitement and interest.

Garibaldi as an impressionable young seaman, before his great exploits began.

The Roots of the Tyneside Music Hall

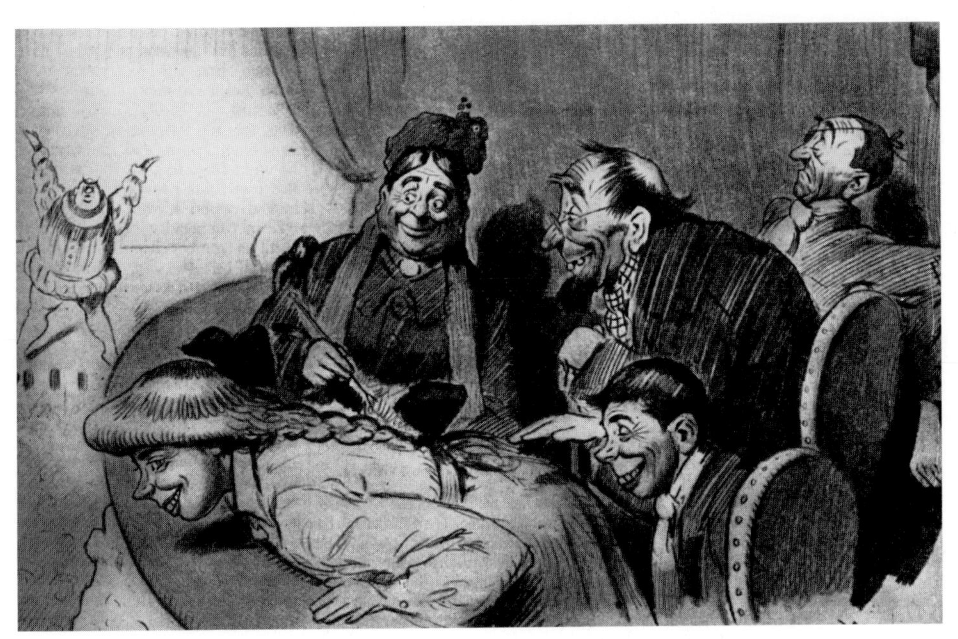

A new 'opium for the masses'; Mr. Punch's view of the Music Hall

The development of the Music Hall was the common man's response to 'high culture' in Victorian times. Having neither the education nor the wherewithal to attend the theatre, opera and ballet, even if they had wanted to, the new 'lower middle classes' and the people who worked for them invented their own equivalent.

Of course, nothing on any large scale was possible until the industrial revolution was well under way and sufficient people had enough money in their pockets to make such a venture pay.

That is why the great age of the Music Hall did not begin until the mid-eighteenth century and sprang to life in mainly urban industrial areas such as Tyneside.

At first, the Music Hall drew very largely on local culture and talent and, in this respect, Tyneside was richly endowed. It is doubtful if any area of the country had as rich a background in local music, distinct humour and outlook as Tyneside. For as far back as could be remembered, the taverns and inns of the waterfront, especially

A Tyneside Wagonway, bearing a 'chauldron' of coal

Newcastle Quayside, had been well served by local bards.

These performers, who earned their living, or at very least the ale to keep them going, by fiddling, singing and reciting, had built up a rich heritage and we still have their songs, even though in many cases we do not even know their names.

Who can now say who wrote that childhood classic, which my own father used to sing to me when I was a toddler, while I delightedly clapped my hands and knees in response;

"Clap your hands for Daddy
Cummin' doon the wagonway,
With a pocket full of pennies
And a bag full of hay."

This song, of course, celebrates the work of the men who drove the tumbrils of coal from the pit-heads down the wooden wagonways to the banks of the Tyne, where the *chauldrons* of 'black diamonds' were loaded on to the keelboats for delivery to the ships. A restored section of wagonway, and one of the tumbrils, can still be seen at Causey Arch, just west of Gateshead.

The keelmen, who frequently indulged in wild drunken 'sprees', were perhaps the principal benefactors and patrons of the local bards and appear in many of those early anonymous tunes, such as *The Keel Row*, to which the Durham Light Infantry still march in double quick-time.

My father, who had served in the Regiment during the war, could hardly keep still whenever he heard it played. "Me legs gan mechanical-like", he used to say!

Ballad singing had always been a feature of

northern life and this tradition filtered down through the Quayside bar singers to feed the Music Hall in its infant years. People on Tyneside have long memories, and traditions die very slowly indeed.

The undoubted animosity which lingers between Tyne and Wear, for instance, dates back to the Civil War of the 1640's and was perpetuated in a ballad sung right up until the Music Hall era in the taverns on Newcastle Quay;

> "Ride through Sandgate, both up and down,
> There ye'll see the gallant lads, fighting for the Crown,
> And all the cull cuckolds of Sunderland Town,
> With the bonny blue caps* cannot pull them down!"
>
> **Scotsmen*

The political uncertainty caused by the nearness of the Scottish border had always made some of the local ballads fraught with meaning, causing many a brawl in the local inns. As late as 1819, during the Great Keelman's Strike, a band struck up *Scots wha hae wi' Wallace bled* on the Town Moor and was promptly arrested by the authorities under the provisions of the Incitement to Riot Act.

The Music Hall, too, drawing on these pungent melodies, must have had its explosive moments in its early days. Proceedings must have been lively at times, to say the least.

One of the earliest contributors to the musical tradition of the Quayside which fed the Tyneside Music Hall was Blind Willie Purvis (1752-1832).

Sandhill, circa 1820

This great performer, beloved by the keelmen whom he entertained all his life, was a master fiddler. Besides that, he was a songwriter and singer of great distinction, rendering his songs with great feeling, in a clear sweet voice and using the highest of keys.

His method of delivery was distinctive. First, someone must buy him ale and place the tankard in his hand. Then he would pledge the health of the King before drinking it off. The King he pledged was George III, whom Blind Willie had heard was "not ower grand". This struck Blind Willie as most tragic, that someone so rich and

Blind Willie

famous could be in ill health. So, as he raised his tankard, he would invariably cry;

"T' the King, God bliss him,
the poor owld sowl!"

Then, the moment the onlookers were waiting for, Blind Willie would begin to slap his knees and stamp. This he did to give his audience the time, before taking up his fiddle to play. Once the tune was going and the audience was with him, he would begin to sing. One can imagine that he often raised the roof. Among his favourites was 'Dance to thy Daddy' but he played the liveliest of tunes and collier's 'rants'. Indeed, he was so popular among his admirers that they compared him to the best that 'high culture' could offer, as can be seen from the following extract;

"Ye gowks that boot daft Handel swarm,
Ya senses jist t' harra,
Styen deff t'strains that maist wad charm
The heart of a wheelbarra,
T'the keeside best repair,
Amang the keelmen pig in
An' hear encored wi' many a blare
Wor ane Blind Willie's singin'."

When Paganini, the world-famous demonic violinist, who was so good that he was thought to have traded his soul to the devil for his talent, visited Newcastle, many rough citizens from the Quayside elbowed their way into the Theatre Royal to see the 'King of the Fiddlers, Baggy Nanny'. Hardly connoisseurs of classical music, however, they were to be disappointed as:

"Divil smash a gud teun cud this bowdykite play,
He cuddint iv pleased me owld granny...."

and they soon found their way back to the Quayside, no doubt to hear their own beloved Blind Willie.

To make money for lodgings and other necessities besides drink, Blind Willie would often hawk rough brooms, heather besoms, which people would buy to sweep their pavements and yards. He adapted and re-arranged an old Scottish song for this, and would go about singing it, by way of 'crying his wares';

The Quayside, in Blind Willie's day

"Buy broom besoms,
Buy them when they're new,
Fine heather besoms,
Better never grew!"

He would add verses as it took his fancy, improvising on life's chances and the events which had befallen him;

"Had ah but a wife, ah care not whie she be,
Be she but a woman, that's enough for me!

If she liked a drop, her an' ah'd agree,
If she didn't like it, aall the mair for me!"

If someone was kind to him, he let people know of it;

"If ye want an oyster, fo' t' taste your mooth,
Call at Handy Walker's, he's a bonny youth."

If not, he lampooned them unmercifully;

"Doon the river side, as far as Dent's Hole,
There ye'll see the cuckolds, working at the coal."

This, again, was a tradition which passed into the Music Hall, where comedians were very topical and trod a very fine line at times. Sometimes, as can be read in newspaper reports of assaults on performers, they were like moths and flew too close to the flame.

Dent's Hole in 1830, complete with 'cuckolds'
(from a contemporary painting by Carmichael)

Blind Willie, of course, was not the only songster working this rich vein, depicting life 'warts and all'. The anonymous writers of collier 'rants', many of which Blind Willie must have sung, produced some marvellous songs such as the one which follows, *Byker Hill*;

"If ah had another penny,
Ah wad hev another gill,
Ah wad ask the piper play,
The Bonny Lass of Byker Hill.

Chorus;

Byker Hill an' Walker Shore,
Collier lads for ever more,
Byker Hill an' Walker Shore,
Collier lads for ever more!

Now when ah forst came here to the dort,
Ah had nee boots an' ah had nee short,
Now ah've gittin two or three,
Man, Walker pit's done well by me!

Geordie Johnson had a pig,
He hit it wi' a shovel an' it danced a jig,
All the way doon Byker Hill,
T' the tune of *Elsie Marley*.

Big Bella she is never yem,
Big Bella she is never here,
When ah calls oot for me suppa,
All ah get's a belted ear!

Now hewin' coal is not fo' sissies,
Hewin' coal is jist fo' men,
If ah had me time back ower,
Ah'd gan back doon the pit again."

Walker Shore in the 1830's, a contemporary engraving

And there are many more verses, some no doubt improvised on the spot to commemorate contemporary events and persons, many of them forgotten and now long gone.

When the colliers held a rant in a tavern, it 'brought the house down'.......literally on occasion! I have read an early nineteenth century newspaper report of a spree at an inn at Dunston to which the terrified landlord was obliged to summon the Watch because "sundry pitmen and keelmen did raise a great dust with their ranting and much damage was threatened to the premises......"

I suppose it's easy to imagine that, if a mob of drunks were stamping uninhibitedly in time to a rant, the floorboards would be moving like a ship in a North Sea gale! Again, this tradition of lively audience participation, welcome or not, became a feature of Music Hall entertainment. People went to the Music Hall to join in!

The story of such a lively gathering as that mentioned above is told in a typical broadside ballad of Henry Robson's, *The Collier's Pay Week*, some extracts of which I give below;

"The baff week is o'er, no repining,
Pay-Saturday's swift on the wing,
At length the blythe morning comes shining,
When kelter makes colliers sing."

The song now describes how the colliers make their way from Benwell into Newcastle and, after some adventures, enter a tavern on the Quay;

"Blind Willie the fiddler sat scrapin',
In a corner jist as they went in,
Some Willington Callants were shaking,
Their feet to his musical din.
Jack vow'd he wad hev some fine cap'ring,
Jist as soon as their dinner was o'er,
Wi' the lassie that wore the white apron,
Now reeling about on the floor."

So, hunger satisfied, he cuts in on the 'Willington Callants' and dances off with the 'frolicsome lass';

"He jumps and his heels knack and rattle,
At the turns of the music so sweet,
He meks such a thundering brattle,
The floor seems afraid of his feet."

And matters get worse for the landlord and his premises when a fight breaks out. Nevertheless, the Benwell lads prevail and throw out the 'Callants', saying scornfully;

"Now, ye collier callants, so clever,
Residing 'tween Tyne and the Wear,
Beware, when ye fuddle together,
Of mekkin' too free wi' strong beer!"

And so the song ends with the usual taunt of the working man at those who "cannot hold their beer"! Of course, what *really* lay behind this skirmish was that the Civil War had been fought all over again!

The 'pamphleteers', or producers of penny broadside ballads, were the second great source of material for the Tyneside Music Hall. Some of these, such as Robert Emery, actually worked for printers, so it was easy and cheap for them to get their work into print.

It will never be known how much of the work printed under their name was actually completely their own and how much was collected around the bars and 'improved' upon by the broadside balladeers, but they certainly deserve our gratitude for at least preserving some great songs.

Robert Emery, in particular, produced some of the best dialect compositions, which, when the Music Hall began, were a great source of comic song. Since he was particularly fond of lampooning the Keelmen and the ignorance of their ways, it would at first seem that the songs must have been produced at considerable risk to his continued good health.

Robert Emery

But a study of contemporary accounts dispels such a fear. It seems that the Keelmen, like modern Irishmen, relished a joke at their own expense and so, though they themselves have now disappeared for ever, we know a great deal about them and their wild, uninhibited ways.

From Emery, for instance, we get the comic classic *Hydrophobia*, which illustrates the Keelmen's rough sense of humour and how they loved to 'take the mickey' out of one another. The first two verses will give the reader a fair idea of the theme:

"When Skipper Carr and Markie Dunn
Were staggerin' drunk through Sandgate,
A dog bit Mark right on the bum
And sair the poor lad found it!
Said Skipper Carr in his voice sae rough,
T' me that dog looked daft enough,
Howway an' git some doctor's stuff,
For fear of Hydrophobia!"

Now the doctor dressed his wounds sae wide
An' left poor Markie smartin',
Then, for a joke, telt Carr aside,
Mark wad gan mad for sartin!
Now Skipper, mind, when on your keel,
Be sure ye watch this Markie weel,
If he begins t' bark an' squeal,
Be sure its Hydrophobia!"

The proposed joke at Markie's expense somehow becomes known to him, however, and he turns the tables on the Skipper, convincing him that he really *has* got the dreaded disease. Barking and howling, he pursues the Skipper around the keel and causes him to leap overboard to escape. Later, appraised of the double-joke, the Skipper is much abashed!

This sort of thing was the very stuff of Music Hall knockabout comedy and one imagines that an all-action tableau could be woven around the song to give it a life of its own.

In addition to *Baggy Nanny*, mentioned earlier, another of Emery's classics was *Jean Jamieson's Ghost*. This song, besides having a beautiful haunting tune, lends itself admirably to the sort of Music Hall melodrama which thrilled and terrified the unsophisticated audience. Jean Jamieson, a fruitseller, was hanged in 1829 on Newcastle Town Moor for killing her mother. She had bashed the poor old soul over the head with a poker whilst in a drunken fit and now haunted the Quayside, near the Sandgate, warning others of the evils of drink;

"The bells of St Ann's they tolled two in the morning,
When bowld Skipper Johnson was gannin to his keel,
From the juice of the barley his poor brain was whorlin',
As he mutt'rin' an' stagg'rin' through San'git did reel.
"No sound could be heard but the keel bullies snorin',
The moon faintly gleamed through the sable clad sky,
When lo, a poor female, her hard fate deplorin',
Appeared at the Pant and thus loudly did cry;

(Chorus)

Fine Chinee oranges, four for a penny,
Lovely ripe cornberries, taste them and try."

Many was the keelman who was momentarily sobered up by this apparition, though we have no means of knowing her long-term effect.

'Jean Jamieson's haunt' by Watts

Keelmen seem to have been the particular victims of vengeful ghosts, judging by yet another of the broadside songs which later became popular on the Music Hall stage.

This song, *Lizzie Mudie's Ghost*, by Willie Armstrong, tells how a skipper, running his keel ignominiously aground at Hebburn Quay Corner, hears mocking laughter from the shore. Leaping off his boat in a rage 'to kill Mr Hoo-Hoo', he soon returns in double quick time, 'pursued by a ghost'!

Again, this must have been marvellous material for what Charlie Chaplin, that great star of the Music Hall at the turn of the century, called a 'comedy tableau'.

Bobby Nunn was another broadside balladeer whose work was ideal to carry over into the Music Hall. His songs were very down to earth and could often be sung raucously by one and all. At very least they had a simple chorus which could be bawled out by the throng. Imagine a packed house participating in Nunn's *Drunken Bella Roy* to the full:

"When Bella's cummin' yem at neet
An' as she's stagg'rin' doon the street,
The bairns cry oot *whie pawned the sheet*?
Wye, drunken Bella Roy-O!

Now if she's had a sup of beer,
She sets t' work t' curse an' swear
An' meks them run away fo' fear
Of drunken Bella Roy-O!

Bella Roy; the author's impression

She'll mek the place like thunder ring
As doon the stairs her things she'll fling,
An' cries *git oot, ye plaguey thing*,
That's drunken Bella Roy-O!

She shoots until she hurts her head
An' then she'll lay doon on her bed,
It's jist a bit of straw doon spread,
For drunken Bella Roy-O!

In her youth, Bella had been a great beauty. People's sense of humour could be extremely cruel in those days.

The third, and final, great source of performers and material from which the early Music Hall on Tyneside could draw was the 'concert party' scene.These shows, sometimes known as 'smokers', were held in rooms hired for the night. Suitable premises were found at church halls, public bars or even just a large room in a private house. Thus, in the great Tyneside song *The Blaydon Races*, we hear that Jackie Broon, the Bellman, was;

"..........talkin' to some cheps,
An' them he was persuadin',
T'gan an' see Geordie Ridley's show,
At the Mechanic's Hall in Blaydon."

A fine piece of self-advertisement if ever I heard one!

Many of the great names of the Music Hall started in such a humble way, with one-man shows held in modest premises before small, but critical, audiences. In fact, no better training for the rough-and-tumble of the Music Hall could be devised than the enforced intimacy of such an act, in such close proximity to the audience.

When the Music Hall proprietors were looking for new acts, it was a simple matter for them to send their 'scouts' round the 'smokers' and pick out the best. Possibly the greatest local songwriter of them all was 'discovered' in this way, the great Joe Wilson, who was 'spotted' performing at a hall in Pelton in December 1864 and engaged immediately for the Balmbara's, mentioned in the *Blaydon Races*.

Of course, Joe Wilson had already been known on the local 'concert party' circuit and to connoisseurs of dialect poetry for some years before his 'big break'. He was another who had worked for a printer and, therefore, had an outlet for his songs, selling them on printed broadsheets for a penny each. In this way, he was already famous for such great classics as *Geordie, haud the bairn, Dinnet Clash the Door* and *The Row upon the Stairs*, which were sung with great gusto around the bars.

Perhaps his best song, however, and certainly the best known, is *Keep Your Feet Still Geordie Hinny*, which I reproduce in full:

"Wor Geordie an' Bob Johnson both laid doon in one bed,
In the little lodgin' hoose that's by the shore.
Wye, they had not been an hour asleep when a kick from Geordie's foot
Made them wekkin' up t' roar instead of snore!

<u>Chorus</u>;

Hey, keep ya feet still Geordie hinny, let's be happy through the neet,
For we may not be sae happy through the day,
So give us that bit comfort, keep your feet still Geordie, lad,
An' divvint drive me bonny dreams away!

Wye ah dreamt there was a dancin' held an' Mary Clark was there
An' ah dreamt ah tripp'd her lightly roond the floor,
An' ah press'd her heavin' breast t' mine as we waltzed aroond the room,
Aye, that's mair than ah hev ever done before!

Joe Wilson sings 'Geordie haud the bairn'

Now, ye all knaa the lad she gans with an' his name is Jimmy Green,
Wye ah dreamt he tried t' spile wor bit of fun,
But ah dreamt ah let 'im have it an' ah blacked the big fyeul's eyes,
If ah'd hev slept ah daint knaa what ah might hev done!

Wye then ah dreamt ah walked her yem that neet an' as we marched alang
Wye ah kissed her lips a thoosand times or mair
An' ah wished the road wad nivvor end, sae happy, like, was ah,
Ah'd hev walked a million miles with Mary then!

Then ah dreamt Jim Green had left the toon an' left his love t' me
An' ah dreamt the hoose was furnished with the best,*
An' ah had jist then left the church wi' Mary on me arm,
When ya bliddy feet completely spiled the rest"

*At this point, the best audiences often roared some such pleasantry as 'all on tick!'

The famous Balmbara's had just come under new management and changed its name to the Oxford Music Hall, so it must have been quite an honour for the young Joe Wilson to be engaged for the opening night.

It was 1865, and Music Halls were well established in the town by then. The first such premises built *specially* for the purpose on Tyneside still exists at No.12, Nelson Street, Newcastle, opposite the Grainger Market. As can be seen from the inscription on the lintel, it was opened in 1838, but it may not have been the first 'Music Hall' to exist.

Many Music Halls evolved on premises used for other purposes and so it is hard to say when they could actually be called a Music Hall, as opposed to other things.

The Balmbara's itself had begun life as the music room of the Wheatsheaf Inn and took its name from the enterprising publican who encouraged and expanded the 'singing room' on the premises. Similarly, one of the most successful Music Halls in South Shields began as the 'singing room' of the Shakespeare Inn, in Union Alley, which used to run parallel to the back of King Street. The publican, Dick Thornton, was an accomplished fiddler who had started out as a busker outside the Marsden Grotto. He probably would not have gotten any further in life except for his determined wife, yet *another* Bella, who pushed and encouraged him all the way. When they were married in 1860 at St Mary's, Gateshead, they only had fourpence ha'penny to their name but when he died in 1922, at the ripe old age of 84, Thornton left £100,000!

Thornton's pub music nights were so successful that they attracted the very best of up-and-coming talent, such as Jimmy Weymis, renowned for his *Lassie Doon on the Quay,* a work of genius, reproduced in full overleaf.

The Lassie Doon on the Quay

Ah'll tell ye of a fine young lass, her name is Sally Gee,
Ah met her in the pub one neet, the pub doon on the Quay,
Ah sez t' her, ah knaa your face, but ah divvint knaa from where
Ah axed her whereaboots she lived an' she sez *oon Carlisle Square.*

Chorus;

Wye never mind, the lassie's kind,
Ah knaa she is good hearted,
She's got a cast in her eye, it meks her look shy
An' ah wish we never had parted.
She's gorra hump an' she walks wi' a stick,
But she's always good t' me,
Ah'm fond o' the lass that nen can pass,
The Lassie doon on the Quay.

It was every neet, ah used t' meet me Sally on the Quay,
Ah axed her wad she marry us, wad she be good t' me?
Now how lang since she's weshed hersell' ah really divvint knaa,
She's got a face like a stotty cake an' she's black as any craa.

It was aall through her, ah took t' drink, ah went from worse t' bad
Ah pawned me watch, ah pawned me chain, an' ivvry thing ah had
An' then one neet, the landlord came an' he hoyed us oot the door
Ah spent six months in Durham Jail wi' me clais put into store.

When the adjoining property, an old woodyard, became vacant, Bella pushed her husband into seizing the opportunity to expand and so 'Thornton's Music Hall' was born, opening for business on the 2nd November, 1885.

At the end of the century, the site was redeveloped again and re-opened as the Empire Palace of Varieties with its grand entrance on King Street. This building can still be seen, as it became the Odeon cinema in 1933 and is now Marks & Spencers store. The 'grand entrance' can still be distinguished too, as the Shoefayre shop.

There had been a Music Hall in South Shields as far back as the 1850's, when Ned Corvan, the famous 'Catgut Jim' took over a pub in Wapping Street and opened 'Corvan's Music Hall'.

His performances were a tremendous success but the business folded since poor old Ned was a bit too fond of the ale! Nevertheless, it was during that era that he wrote one of the most famous comic songs of all time, one which brought a dubious fame to the town of Hartlepool.

The song *The Fishermen Hung the Monkey-O!* (a harrowing extract from which follows) can still get you a black eye in Hartlepool down to the present day.

The Fishermen Hung the Monkey-O!

In former times, mid war an’ strife,
When French invasion threatened life,
An’ all was armed up t’ the knife,
The fishermen hung the monkey-o!
The fishermen, wi’ courage high,
Seized the monkey for a spy,
Hang him says yen, for he must die,
They did, and hung the monkey-o!

They tried all means t’ mek him speak,
They tortured him ’til he did squeak,
That’s French, says yen, another Greek,
And the fishermen then got drunkey-o!
He’s all o’er hair some cheps did cry,
He’s up t’ summick cute an’ sly,
Wiv a cod’s heed they closed his eye,
Afore they hung the monkey-o!

Now let us hope that ever at sea,
We’ll still maintain sovirinity
May France and England long agree,
And nivvor at each get funkey-o!
Regards poor pug ah’ve had me say,
His times they’ve past for mony a day,
But in Hartlepool, thoo’ll hear lads say;

(LOUDLY)
WHIE HUNG THE MONKEY-O?

Corvan as ‘Catgut Jim’

Actually, the idea was not original and Ned, as I suspect did many of the 'broadside balladeers', merely 'improved' on an existing song. Compare these lines from Willie Armstrong's *Baboon*, which was written before Ned Corvan was born;

"Sum time since, some wild beasts thor cam t' the toon
An' in the collecshun a famous baboon,
In uniform dressed, if my story ye're willin',
Gat loose iv its captors an' ran t' High Fellin'"

The poor creature encounters three pitmen and;

"Tom flung doon his pipe an' set up a greet yell,
He's either a spy or Owld Boney hissell',
In a crack the whole toon was in full hue and cry,
T' ketch Boney-part or the hairy French spy!

The 'hairy French spy'

Another product of the hard school of clubs and 'concert parties' was Geordie Ridley, author of Tyneside's adopted anthem *The Blaydon Races*. After a pit accident sustained at an early age, he had been forced to use his musical talents in order to make a living. In common with many Tynesiders in those hard times, he had started work at the age of eight but, whilst serving as a wagon-rider, the lad had fallen off and been crushed by the train. Paid off crippled, he began busking and singing around the clubs and bars, writing his own songs, clawing his way to local fame.

Eventually making his Music Hall debut at the Grainger Music Hall, he no doubt would have gone on to even greater fame had he not died in 1864, succumbing to his pit injuries at only thirty years of age. Contemporary records speak of his fine voice' but, in particular, praise his 'powers of mimickry' which 'swayed his audience at will'. This skill, honed in the packed atmosphere of the 'smoker' and 'concert party', stood him in good stead on the Music Hall stage. Many of his songs lend themselves to 'a little bit of pantomine', but none more so than *Cushy Butterfield,* that marvellous burlesque which, apart from *Blaydon Races*, was the song which won him undying fame.

In fact, quite a few of Ridley's songs parodied local 'characters' but not everyone was as willing as the Keelmen to enjoy a joke at their own expense.

After the first performance of *Cushy Butterfield*, the bard had to go into hiding for over a month to avoid the 'muckman' Tom Grey, who threatened to 'stot his heed' when he laid hands on him for maligning his cousin in such a hilarious way.

Cushy Butterfield

"Ah'm a broken-hearted keelman and ah'm ower heed in love
With a young lass from Gatesheed an' ah calls her me dove,
Her name's Cushy Butterfield an' she sells yella clay,
An' her cousin is the muckman an' they calls him Tom Grey.

Chorus;

She's a big lass, she's a bonny lass, an' she likes her beer,
An' ah calls her Cushie Butterfield an' ah wish she was here.

Ye'll oft see her doon Sangit when the fresh herrin' comes in
She's like a bag-full of sawdust tied roond wiv a bit string
An' she wears big galoshes too an' her stockings once was white,
Wiv her bedgoon of leylock an' her hat's nivvor strite.

Now her eyes are like two holes in a blanket burned through
An' her breath in the mornin' wad stun a young cow,
But when ah hear her a-gollarin' WILL YE BUY ONY CLAY?
Like the candyman's trumpet, it steals me young heart away.

When ah telt her that ah loved her, she started t' laff
(here the singer giggles)
She says nen of ya monkey-stuff, cos ah divvint like such chaff.
But then ah axed her t' marry us an' she ROARED LIKE A BULL
An' the lads on the keel says ah's nowt but a fyeul!

She says the lad that wad marry us, he'll hev t' work every day,
Aye, an' when he cums back yem at neet, he'll hev t' gang an' seek clay,
Aye, an' when he's oot there seekin' it, ah'll mek balls an' sing,
Oh, weel may the keel row that my laddie's in!

Now the method of delivery of this great song was (and is) as important as the lyrics. The words printed in block capitals were delivered between cupped hands to give great volume, in true imitation of the delicate maid, while the words which immediately followed were rendered in a sort of quivering falsetto. The comic effect was stunning. This was Music Hall at its very best and there were few who could match Ridley on his day.

Of course, there were those who didn't want to, like Tommy Armstrong, the 'pitman's poet' whose work became tremendously popular in the Music Halls, whilst he himself steadfastly refused to 'graduate' to the bigger stage.Other artistes sang his songs such as *Aye, Wor Nanny's a Maisor*, *There's nee gud luck in Durham Jail* and *Stanley Market*, but, if you wanted to hear the bow-legged little man himself, you had to go to the local pubs or Miner's Halls.

There is no doubt that many other areas in the United Kingdom had their own musical tradition upon which the budding Music Hall was able to draw.

In Arnold Bennett's *Five Towns* novels for instance, the local entertainers of the Potteries, with their dialect songs and clog-dancing, are graphically described.

But none could match Tyneside and it is quite possible that Music Halls were introduced earliest in *this* area, despite the claims of Lambeth's Canterbury Hall (opened in 1849) to be the 'father of all Music Halls'.

The Tyneside Music Halls were not just among the earliest, but were the most firmly rooted in the traditions of the local people. Able to draw upon a virtual 'gold mine' of local resources, no material was required from elsewhere.

Goodbye, but don't forget us!

When the 'Makems' showed the way

250hp oscillating engines for HMS 'Salkeld' (from 'The Engineer', 1872)
It can be seen that marine engines were becoming sophisticated and the men who built them were beginning to realise their own worth

The North Eastern Engineers' strike of 1871 was one of the most important events in British industrial history. It was also a very remarkable action insofar as, although many of the strikers were members of trade unions, the strike was *not* union-led or organised, but sprang from the spontaneous feelings of the men. It was, in modern terms, an 'unofficial' dispute.

The purpose of the strike was to secure a reduction in working hours from an average of ten hours to nine per day, and thus a reduction of the working week from sixty hours to fifty-four. The demand was not out of keeping with the spirit of the times, a national 'nine hour' movement having been established in 1870 to publicise and agitate for the workers' right to more recreation time. The first phase of the industrial revolution was beginning to wind down and the workers, many of whom had been newly enfranchised, were starting to realise that they were worth more than just a subsistence wage. They wanted not just the means but also the time to enjoy their leisure.

The outcome of the strike was possibly of more importance to the future of the ordinary working people of the United Kingdom than any other industrial dispute, before or after.

On Saturday, 25th March 1871, seven to eight hundred men employed in the engineering trade on the River Wear met at the Theatre Royal, Sunderland, to discuss the possibility of approaching their employers with a request for the introduction of the nine-hour working day. Besides actual engineers, the men included boilermakers, iron moulders, blacksmiths, plumbers, pattern-makers, brass-founders and finishers among their number. These were all the essential trades in the iron-shipbuilding industry.

The result of the meeting was that a petition was framed and presented to the "masters" respectfully requesting that the new working hours be introduced in the week commencing the 3rd of April. The masters peremptorily refused, posting notices to that effect in their works on Friday, 31st March, and reminding the men of their contractual obligations. The stage was thus set for one of the most momentous and significant struggles in British working-class history.

Sans Street Assembly Hall, where most of the strike meetings were held. Built as a Wesleyan Chapel in 1793, it survived as a Mission Hall until 1963.

photo by permission of Alton Pickersgill

The day after the masters' emphatic refusal of their petition, the men met at the Assembly Hall, Sans Street, Sunderland. With over a thousand present, the atmosphere of the meeting, though orderly, was militant.

J. Strothers, a pattern-maker, took the chair and, after many rousing and determined speeches, it was resolved that a walk-out would be staged on Monday, 3rd April, the very day on which the men had requested the new working hours to commence.

A further resolution from the floor, moved by Andrew Gourley, proposed that, should there be any 'blacklegs', there would be no return to work until such traitors were dismissed.

Over five years previously, Gourley had figured prominently in a dispute at the Jarrow works of Charles Palmer and had seen the resolution of his workmates crumble and the strike collapse. This time there must be no lack of solidarity and no shirking the task!

Perhaps because of the firmness of the men's resolve, the walkout had immediate results. That very afternoon, as more than 2000 men met on Sunderland Town Moor to roar out their approval for the strike, three firms capitulated and unconditionally granted the reduction in hours demanded. These firms, Tyzack Bell, E. Bailey and Thew the Brassmonger, were small and could not afford to lose production for even a short period of time.

Actually, even the bigger firms were in little better condition to resist the strike. As the editorial of the *Shields Gazette* pointed out on the following day, the men had timed their action impeccably, the "demand for marine engines being brisk". Indeed, the men could have "no better opportunity" to press their claims since the "purchase of steamers (was) only limited by the capacity for the production of their engines".

The editor made it plain that he thought the men were taking unfair advantage and suggested that their action "will not tend to commend trade unions to general favour". It seemed that the editor was unaware that the action was spontaneous, rather than union-led, and included many non-unionists among the strikers.

In conclusion, the editor remarked that "it will be a public misfortune if the employers give way" to the "ultimatum of those who thereby seek to reverse the natural order of things by putting the shoulders of the industrial body above its head". But, even as the newspaper appeared on the streets, four firms gave way, including the Wear Commissioners, employers of no less than 300

Strikers gather on the High Street
(Illustration by permission of A. Pickersgill)

men and boys. The others were Adamson (30 employees), Crowley (25) and Cogden (20).

Firms employing a total of over 500 men had now given way, but the masters were by no means beaten. Through the columns of the newspapers, they began to threaten legal action for breach of contract against the strikers who had left them 'high and dry' with their order books full.

Well aware that they must avoid confrontation with the law, the strikers strove to keep order in their ranks during those early days of the dispute. This was no easy task, so many angry men being thrown into idleness, to hang about on the streets, a prey to gossip and rumour. Nevertheless, even the newspapers had to concede that the crowds were orderly, except for the apprentice boys, who caused a disturbance one afternoon outside the Golden Lion pub in Sunderland High Street.

'The Golden Lion' shortly before its demolition in recent years
(Photo by permission A Pickersgill)

Rather more serious was the case of George Cockburn, who assaulted a 'blackleg', Frederick Gale, on the day after the strike began. Actually, the suggestion was made in court that Cockburn had a personal motive in attacking Gale, who had bragged that he could 'go with' his assailant's wife. But this was the sort of incident, with its attendant bad publicity, which the strikers could ill afford.

On Saturday the 8th April, the editor of the *Shields Gazette* tried a new tactic to break the strike, calling for an immediate ballot of the men since "the strike hands must be pretty well aware, as public opinion is dead set against them, that the

Sunderland High Street at the time of the strike
(Illustration by kind permission of Alton Pickersgill)

chances of a victory against the masters is but small". Indeed, went on the editor, if a ballot *had* been held authorising the strike action, the masters would have listened, but the men had been 'unwisely' advised.

A further attempt to shake the men's solidarity through the press was made in a letter to the *Sunderland Herald* by Mr W.S Lindsay, who had formerly been the town's Member of Parliament. This letter pointed out that the action of the men in striking was "merely giving advantage to competitors". Following this letter, however, came an admission by the editor that he had received several letters in *support* of the strike, but he had chosen not to print them as their "spirit and tone render their publication a misdemeanour".

At mass meetings held on the 12th and 13th April, the men ignored this rather obvious attempt to drive a wedge between themselves and their leaders, voting to press on with their demand for the nine-hour day without concessions. A denial was issued from the platform that the men "already lack food" and a resolution was accepted from the floor congratulating the citizens of Sunderland on having gotten rid of Mr. Lindsay as their representative in Parliament.

As to their competitors, it was pointed out that in the USA engineers worked only *eight* hours per day and their industry was certainly no less competitive.

The *Sunderland Herald* of the 14th April carried more news of what the editor referred to as the "unfortunate difficulty" of the strike in the engineering trades. Mr Oswald, the shipbuilder, had declined to give his men the wages which were due to them at the beginning of the walkout, pointing out that *they* had broken their contract, not himself. He would gladly hand over any money due to the men if they would return and work their contracted notice. Also, on the same day, it was reported that four strikers were being brought before the magistrates to answer charges of breach of contract to their employer, George Clark, of Monkwearmouth Engine Works.

All four, boilermaker Thomas Barclay and fitters George Lumsden, H. Rattenby and Alex Pattison, were found guilty and ordered to pay compensation of £1 each. The men refused to accept the verdict and exercised their right to appeal to a higher court, citing lack of evidence as their grounds.

The Candlish Memorial in Sunderland
Despite his popularity and reputation as a radical, he did nothing to help the strikers

Newly arrived from London, the town's latest Member of Parliament, John Candlish, decided that it was time he took the matter in hand. It seems incredible, by modern standards, that he began his speech with the admission "it is twelve months

Engine works machine shops. These are actually those of Jarrow Palmers, where strike leader Andrew Gourley had once worked.

since I have had the honour and pleasure of meeting my constituents", before going on to urge all sides to submit their differences to arbitration.

The opinions of this most popular man, who had once been described by Mr Gladstone as "one of the most fearless and independent members of the House of Commons", might well have been expected to carry more weight, had his neutrality not been cast in doubt by the position he held as a commissioner of the River Wear Navigation.

Furthermore, barely had he issued his appeal than it was announced that Mr Oswald, shipbuilder, was intending to serve 200 of his striking workers with a summons. In the event, Mr Oswald called only 35 to account, but his ill-timed gesture seems to have had no other effect than to harden the strikers' resolve.

At a meeting on the 19th April, the strikers decided to send delegates to the engineers of the Tyne in a confident attempt to enlist their help and thus widen the dispute.

Shipyard brass foundry.
All trades were involved in the strike, including the brass-foundrymen

Mr Candlish's advice was debated and rejected, since there was a widely-held belief that arbitration usually 'split the difference' between disputants. The men were determined to settle for nothing less than the nine-hour day.

On the following day, fully cognisant that the men had rejected it, the employers attempted to take the moral high ground by offering arbitration. Another stalemate having been reached, the Wearside engineers held their breath, awaiting the decision of the men of the Tyne.

Irrespective of any outside help, however, the solidarity of the men was having its effect. The editor of the *Sunderland Herald* was forced to report that the situation "remains unaltered, notwithstanding the position of the magistrates" whilst "everything connected with the engineering trade in this port is at a standstill".

On the 22nd April 1871, the very morning of the Tyneside engineers' meeting to consider the Wearsiders' request, the editorials of the local newspapers earnestly expressed the hope that "they will not follow the example of the engineers of the Wear, with whom it was only a word and a blow" and would deal "honourably" with their employers, giving due notice if any action was contemplated.

A typical shipyard of the time, engraved by W. J. Palmer
It can be see that, whether the ships were built of iron or not, the joiner's work was still essential

Perhaps influenced by this advice, but more likely by the age-old antipathy between Tyne and Wear, the Newcastle and Gateshead men did *not* agree to immediately down tools and join the strike. Whilst sending their 'cordial sympathy' to the strikers on the Wear, the Tyneside men favoured arbitration and would ask for it to apply to the whole of the North Eastern district. Indeed, the Tynesiders criticised the Sunderland men for striking without warning and thought them to have been 'hasty' in their actions. They, too, wanted the nine-hour day, but they would petition for it in an orderly fashion. Meanwhile, they promised to support the Sunderland strikers in all *legal* ways.

Just as this disappointing response was reported back to the Wearside men, however, their cause received a massive boost by the capitulation of the litigious Mr Oswald, whose shipbuilding facility was, in the woestruck words of the local newspapers, "one of the principal and largest establishments on the banks of the Wear", employing over 500 engineers.

Mr Oswald, who had also been beset by a strike of joiners at his yard, could no longer hold out and granted the nine-hour day without conditions. At the same time, Mr Nelson of Monkwearmouth, who employed 30 to 40 hands, gave in to his employees. More than 1000 had now returned victoriously to work on the Wear, and definite cracks were appearing in the employers' dam. It seemed that the Wearside engineers could win the nine-hour day without any help from the Tyne.

Thus, on Monday 24th April, when the crowded meeting at Sans Street Assembly Hall was told of the Tynesiders' decision, they were adamant in their renewed rejection of arbitration. In fact, the proposer of this compromise, Mr Cordingly, was howled down with cries of "nothing to arbitrate" and "put him out". Furthermore, despite their cool reception of the Wearsiders' pleas and their faith in arbitration, it was now certain that the Tyneside engineers were, after all, set to join the strike. The rich, powerful Tyneside employers, having been given time and warning, had organised themselves much more effectively than their Wearside counterparts and were uncompromising in their refusal of their employees' petitions. The widening of the dispute, far from being an advantage, now began to look like a liability to the strikers.

It now became particularly important that the Wearside men conclude their dispute, before these much more resolute opponents appeared in the lists and gave their masters the chance to renege on their promises.

It was with great fury, therefore, that the men learned that a temporising lifeline had been cast to the employers from an unlikely source. The strikers' leaders were informed by letter that, uninvited, the Amalgamated Engineers Society had 'negotiated a settlement' on their behalf. Messrs Allen and Austin, officials of the union, of which less than 25% of the strikers were members, had met with the employers and agreed that the men would return to work on the old terms, provided that the nine-hour day was granted to them from the first week in June. Of

The 'interfering' Mr Allen

course, the danger of allowing the employers such a respite in which to re-organise was immediately recognised by all but the interfering Messrs. Allen and Austin, who only seemed intent on claiming some credit for their union in settling the strike.

At a packed meeting at the Assembly Hall, "the nice little business that had been done for them by these two gentlemen" was roundly condemned by the enraged strikers. Their "unwarranted interference" was considered "a piece of impudence", especially by the non-union majority, and when a vote of censure was proposed "a forest of hands was held up for it among loud applause".

The men voted for a continuation of the strike and the employers were left in no doubt that "nine hours pure and simple", to take *immediate* effect, were the only terms on which the strike would end. No doubt bitterly, the remark was made from the platform that they "all would now be back at work if everybody had minded their own business".

Nevertheless, this was the last event of the strike. The employers, desperate to settle, capitulated completely, and the newspapers of the 3rd May, 1871 carried the tidings that the men had returned to work on their own, not the union's terms.

The editor of the *Shields Gazette*, fully recognising the importance of the event, summed up admirably with the following report:

> "The strike.....on the result of which so many interests in this district may be said to hang, has now come to a close, the turn-outs having succeeded in gaining their point by the limitation of their period of daily labour to nine hours. Indefensible as was the conduct of the men in leaving their employment without tendering even a day's notice, they must still be credited with having manifested far more capability in the management of their affairs than their ill-used masters, who have not only shifted their ground, but also weakened their position by the want of unaniminity amongst themselves......If the employers of Sunderland cannot manage......they had much better put their affairs into commission, and call at the *Golden Lion* for instruction from the triumphant Lords of Labour."

Four days later, the *Sunderland Herald* announced that "the mania for striking amongst the trades in Sunderland appears to have become an epidemic. Engineers, ship joiners, glassmakers, now *underhands*.......who comprise the very lowest form of unskilled labour in the iron shipbuilding yards" were demanding the limitation of the working day to nine hours.

Victorian employers might well have wondered where it would all end, this movement that the working men of Sunderland had started.

Postscript

The Tyneside men, who had been so 'honourable' in their dealings with their masters, won their strike too, though their fight was much longer and bloodier, and their victory was much less conclusive.

Though it is true that the Tyneside men faced the more formidable opposition, and that their strike was more widely known, being given national coverage by such eminent publications as the 'London Illustrated News', it is nevertheless a fact that the Sunderland men *were* the first to win the nine-hour day.

The Nine-Hours League, which had until then met with only limited success in minor trades, had been looking for a 'big strike' in a major industry. The Sunderland men had the courage to take up that challenge, a fact generously acknowledged by D. C. Cummings, General Secretary of the Boilermaker's Union.

Writing in 1905, besides admitting that the winning of the nine-hour day had been a "victory of the rank and file" and "not the union leaders", he went on to say that it was "commencing with a strike of engineers in *Sunderland*" that the cause had been won.

D. C. Cummings

Palmers' Warships

The Monument to Sir Charles Mark Palmer, Bart., M.P.
Presently (2001) located near the entrance to the Tyne Pedestrian Tunnel, overlooking the river.

Charles Mark Palmer, the man who was once described as the 'founder' of modern Jarrow (the old town was barely more than a village before his time), was born in King Street, South Shields on the 3rd November, 1822. He was the fourth son of a local timber merchant, George Palmer, and enjoyed a very comfortable childhood and a sound education, attending Dr Bruce's Academy, in Percy Street, Newcastle, before completing his studies abroad, in Marseille.

After serving his business apprenticeship with Messrs Redshaw and Ridley, he joined his father's firm. Further valuable experience was gained in partnership with the pit-owner, John Bowes, before he entered the shipbuilding business.

In 1851, together with his elder brother George, the young entrepreneur bought a shipyard at Jarrow and commenced to build iron ships. When his brother retired from the business in 1862, Charles Mark was left in sole charge and, despite turning the business into a public company in 1865, so he remained, as Chairman and Managing Director, until his retirement in 1893. When he died at his rented town house in Curzon Street, London, on the 4th June, 1907, he left an estate of only £15,226. Never afraid to trust his own judgement, he had built his business empire entirely on borrowed capital.

On April the 24th, 1856, huge crowds gathered on both sides of the Tyne to witness the launch of Palmers' first naval vessel, the 'ironclad' *Terror*. The Jarrow shipyard had made a prodigious effort to turn the vessel out in just over four months, but she was launched too late to ever see action. The Crimean War, which had prompted the Admiralty to order her building, had ended less than a month previously and the huge vessel, which was more of a floating gun battery than a warship, was redundant before completion.

Palmers' First Warship; HMS 'Terror' at Sea

Nevertheless, she had proven to the world how quickly British industry could respond to a challenge and this was possibly of more importance in the long run than her participation in any actual conflict.

For many years the Admiralty had been sceptical about the usefulness of iron in warship construction. Tests carried out in the 1840s had shown that the brittle metal which was all that was available at the time was far from proof against gunnery. In fact, the forged iron plates split into many lethal shards on impact and this was even more dangerous to crew members than splinters of wood, the traditional scourge of the gundeck in sea battles of the Napoleonic Wars.

The 'Terror' on the stocks at Jarrow, 1856

Having once tested and rejected the metal, the Admiralty continued stubbornly to ignore advances made by forgemasters until the French, who were our allies in the Crimean conflict but our rivals in the wider world of international politics, demonstrated once and for all the defensive capabilities of iron plating.

The 'ironclad' gun batteries which they had built for the Crimean War sailed right up to the Russian Black Sea fortress of Kinburn and, impervious to the enemy's bombardment, reduced their fortifications to rubble.

The world took note, and not least of all the British Admiralty. If the 'wooden walls of England' were to remain proof against future enemies, they would have to be clad with iron!

The Battle of Kinburn took place in October 1855, and before the year was out the Admiralty had reacted to restore British Naval supremacy. Quite rightly, it was judged that civilian shipyards had more expertise in iron-ship construction than the Naval Dockyard at Portsmouth, so orders for four 'ironclads' were placed with civilian yards. The orders were deliberately placed at different yards, so as to ensure that all four vessels would be ready for action as quickly as possible. Not surprisingly, Palmers of Jarrow, who had recently stunned the shipping world and revolutionised the east coast coal-carrying trade with their iron-screw colliers, were allocated one of the orders.

Work on the *Terror*, as Palmers' vessel was to be known, commenced on the 7th January, 1856, and more than 1000 laboured daily to build the huge vessel.

Realising the vital national importance (and, quite possibly, the potential for further orders) of the commission, Palmers suspended all other work at the yard and, as reported by the *Shields Gazette*, "laboured with all their force on the immense iron battery". On launch day, the *Gazette* emphasised the staggering expediency of Palmers' work by giving the following dimensions of the *Terror*:

> She was 185 ft (60 metres) long, 48 ft 6in (15 metres) in the beam and 18ft 6in(6 metres) deep, displacing almost 2000 tons when in the water.

Local wags joked that they expected her to "tek aall the water oot the Tyne" and, at her launching, shouted "stand by for a tidal wave!" across the river to the spectators in Howdon.

The *Gazette* further reported that she was "spoon-bowed, framed and plated like an ordinary iron ship" (not that many outside of Tyneside knew what an 'ordinary' iron ship looked like!) but, outside her plating, she carried a sheath of armour four inches (10cm) thick, mounted on to teak a further six inches (15cm) in thickness. She carried an armament of thirty 68lb muzzle-loading guns and, to enable her to operate in shallow waters, was of flat-bottomed construction.

Her 200hp Napier engines, however, were sufficient only for battle manouevres. On sea passages, she would have to be towed to her destination. Nevertheless, it was obvious to all concerned that, once on station, she would be a formidable fighting machine!

The *Terror* was named by Mrs George Palmer and, despite her bulk and the comments of the wags, the newspapers unanimously agreed that she slid into the water gracefully on launch day.

Fitting out was rapid and, just three days after her launch, she was towed out of the Tyne by the screw steamers *Alice* and *Warrior*, with local steam tug *Royal Albert* in attendance, bound for Sheerness to be commissioned into the Royal Navy.

She was never to fire a shot in anger, however, being sent to Hamilton, Bermuda, where she spent her days acting as a commissioning base until finally being scrapped in 1903.

Her armour plating was never tested in action, which was a great pity, for the ever-innovative Charles Palmer had conceived the idea of *rolling* her plates instead of forging them, a process which he was certain would make them far more resistant to impact.

The following extract from an address to the British Association by Charles Mark Palmer at Newcastle in 1863, demonstrates Palmers' efforts in this respect and how reluctant the Admiralty were to adopt new ideas, or even to incur any expenditure in testing them:

> "It was in the building of this vessel (*The Terror*) that rolled armour plates were first used......To the use of these rolled plates, however, the Admiralty opposed itself; but we feeling

Palmers' Iron & Steel Works, where the revolutionary plates were rolled

convinced, by experiments which we made, that the rolled armour plates were at least equal to the forged, invited the Admiralty to a trial of their efficiency.

"We built a target nine feet square, on a plan which we thought might be advantageously adopted for large vessels of war, and on the cellular principle. The cells we filled with compressed cotton, which we had found by experiment to be very effectual in stopping shot. On this target was a thin teak backing; on the teak were bolted one hammered and two rolled plates. The target was bolted on to the side of an old wooden frigate at Portsmouth, under the direction of Captain Hewlett.

"The firing showed that, whilst the hammered plate split and cracked to pieces, the rolled plates were not broken, only indented, and were superior to the hammered plate in every respect.

"Unfortunately, the target was not firmly bolted to the vessel, and it sprung at every shot, so that the bolts which held the armoured plates were broken, and they fell into the sea.

"A shot was then tried to test the resisting power of the compressed cotton, and it appeared to answer so well that Captain Hewlett advised a series of experiments to be tried.

"The Admiralty were willing, but required us to provide the targets at our own expense. Having already spent upwards of £1000 on experiments for the good of the country, we

HMS 'Defence'; She temporarily cost Palmers their reputation

declined this proposal; nevertheless, we had proved to the Admiralty this important fact, that the rolled plates were superior to the forged, and they have since been universally adopted.

"We claim, therefore, for this district the honour of being the first to prove the strength and utility of rolled armour plates, since known and spoken of in Parliament as *Palmers' Rolled Plates.*"

As it was, the utility and importance of Palmer's idea did eventually become well known and became standard practice in warship design, but an early demonstration of the effectiveness of 'Palmers' rolled plates' would have been greatly advantageous to the Jarrow yard, which now had to wait over five years before winning another 'capital ship' order for the Royal Navy. Not that many large naval vessels were being built at that time. As always in times of peace, funds for naval development became scarce in the period following the Crimean War. Only three 'ironclads' were ordered in the next five years, the *Warrior*, the *Black Prince* and the *Defence*, the last of these commissions being awarded to Palmers. The order was placed in 1861, a launch date of 2nd January 1862 being stipulated in the contract.

Palmers failed to meet the deadline and learned a valuable lesson from their failure. As with most steam-powered vessels of the time, in addition to her engine power the ship was to be fully rigged as a sailing frigate, and Palmers had sub-contracted the fabrication of the masts to the Thames Ironworks. When the launch date fell due, the hull was ready but the masts had not yet even left the London river.

Palmers' Integrated Works, c1880.

The Admiralty despatched their commissioners north to enquire into the causes of the delay, which, if they would but believe it, lay on their own doorstep. A written report was demanded as to why the vessel would not now be ready before mid-January, and Palmers' hitherto unblemished reputation was badly damaged.

Charles Mark Palmer, who had by then taken full charge of the company on the retirement of his older brother George, determined on a typically daring solution to ensure that Palmers was never to be blamed again for the failure of others.

By 1865, he had expanded the capital available to the yard enormously by launching it as a limited liability company. With the financial backing so created, he laid down plans for the world's first fully-integrated shipbuilding complex. In future, Palmers would build not just the ships, their rigging and their engines, but would produce the very iron from which they would be constructed.

Eventually, it was to be truly said of Palmers that they were the only company in the world who could take in raw iron ore (from their own mines) at one end of the works and turn out a completed ship at the other!

Palmers' failure to meet the deadline for the launching of the *Defence* was not the only bad news to affect 'ironclad' production in 1862. Doubts about the whole concept of such vessels had been renewed by the poor sea-keeping

HMS 'Warrior' at Hartlepool, after being restored to her former glory

qualities of the *Warrior.* In early February, 1862, on a voyage to Lisbon, she had almost foundered and had only with great difficulty been made to answer her helm.

The *Shields Gazette* of 11th February 1862 carried a report of the potentially disastrous voyage and, in the following days, printed many letters from the general public expressing doubts as to whether these iron monsters represented value for money after all. Cutting such a poor figure in contrast to the graceful 'tall ships' of the previous era, of course, it is hardly surprising that the appearance of the 'ironclads' appalled many traditionalists.

Ironically enough, however, though the public was not to know it, the *Warrior* was not only to weather the storms (literal and literary), but to provide useful service for over a century! In 1904, she was converted into a power plant for the Royal Naval Torpedo School and in 1929, reduced to a hulk, she became a jetty for ships refuelling at the Milford Haven Depot, where she remained until 1979. Some value for money!

In 1979, her historical value being at last appreciated, the *Warrior* was towed to Hartlepool where, in an eight-year project, she was restored, as near as possible, to her original condition by North Eastern shipbuilding craftsmen. She now lies at the Portsmouth Dockyard Museum, alongside Nelson's flagship *Victory* and Henry VIII's *Mary Rose*.

And what of Palmers? After their failure to meet the deadline for the delivery of the *Defence*, they had to wait ten years before the Royal Navy entrusted them with another contract for a 'capital ship'. But then, during the aftermath of the Franco-Prussian War and the emergence of Germany as a serious threat to world peace, orders for no fewer than *four* 'ironclads' were placed with the Jarrow shipyard.

This time, relying on no-one else to fulfil their contracts, Palmers made no mistake in delivering the work on time. All four vessels rolled off the stocks during the eventful year of 1872, the new integrated complex turning out the ships like a production line. It was said on Tyneside that Palmers built ships 'by the yard' and, from that time onwards, there was to be no shortage of naval contracts.

Their reputation fully restored, they were to produce vessels of every type and size for the Royal Navy, turning out over a hundred before the end of the First World War. Each time a new type of vessel was required, or a new need was perceived by the Admiralty in the defence of the nation's interests, Palmers were sure to be allocated their share of the work.

During the 1870s, for instance, the period in which overseas territories were being added to the Empire in the Far East and along the coasts of West Africa, the need was for vessels which could operate close inshore and penetrate the creeks and tropical rivers. Palmers were called upon to supply a class of river gunboat, and their initial design was so successful that no fewer than a dozen were ordered by the Admiralty in the two years 1875 to 1876.

As new weapons were developed, Palmers were among the first of shipbuilding companies to be called upon by the Admiralty to respond. In January 1878, when the Russian warship *Constantine* proved to the world the effectiveness of Whitehead's torpedo by sinking a Turkish

Men at work in Palmers' forge

steamer off Batoum during the Turco-Russian War, orders were immediately placed with the Jarrow yard for a new class of vessel capable of launching the deadly missiles.

Once again, Palmers came up with a winning design, so much so that *ten* of the vessels, to be known as 'Torpedo Miners', were to be ordered and supplied to the Admiralty over the next three years.

In later years, the 'Torpedo Miners' became so effective in naval warfare that it was necessary to design a completely new class of vessel with the speed and manoeuvrability to counteract them. Again, Palmers participated fully in the production of this new type of ship, the 'Torpedo

HMS 'Star', one of the earliest class of 'Destroyer' built by Palmers

Boat Destroyer', later to be simply named the 'Destroyer'.

The salient feature of these vessels was their tremendous engine power, and here the Jarrow yard, with their own integrated engine shop, had the edge over their rivals thanks to the foresight of their founder, the now-knighted Sir Charles Mark Palmer. Over the years from 1895 until the end of the First World War, Palmers supplied no fewer than eight classes of this new type of vessel, a total of 44 ships in all, with engine power rated up to 27,000hp.

Palmers' engine works were also to supply the first triple-expansion steam engines to be fitted to a warship when, in 1888, the cruisers *Orlando* and *Undaunted* were built at the Jarrow complex.

The durability of Palmers' vessels was also well-known and respected. Even in the highly-competitive world of warship production, when designs were sometimes obsolete even before the vessels were completed, Palmers' ships stood the test.

Proof lies in the fact that the oldest 'capital ship'

HMS 'Revenge' leaves Palmers; a wonderfully atmospheric painting by marine artist Lund.

to actually fight in the First World War was the battleship *Revenge*, built at Palmers in 1893, over 20 years before the outbreak of hostilities. Re-armed, refitted and renamed *Redoubtable* (another *Revenge* was already on the stocks at Vickers of Barrow at the outbreak of war and was commissioned in 1916), Palmers' old ship took part in the bombardment of the enemy's coastal defence works and trenches in Belgium.

Hardly younger was Palmers' cruiser *Pegasus*, built in 1898. She did sterling service off the East African coast as part of Rear Admiral King-Hall's squadron, destroying the enemy's communication stations, until she herself was caught and destroyed by the *Koenigsberg* whilst cleaning her boilers off Zanzibar. Helplessly immobile and hopelessly outgunned by the much more modern German cruiser, she was sunk with the loss of 33 killed and 59 wounded, out of a complement of 234, according to the casualty list printed in the *Shields Gazette* of the 22nd September 1914.

HMS 'Pegasus', built 1898 and sunk by enemy action at Zanzibar, 1914

The engine room took the bulk of the casualties and the dreadful list included the following men with local connections;

Lt. Cmdr. R.C. Turner;
Lt. J. J. H. Drake, RNR;
P.O. E. Horrill, Highams, Rowberry;
A.B. Hodgetts, James Smith, Vaughan
O.S. Burns, Wright;
Chief Engineroom Artificer Glanville;
Stoker P.O. Cole;
Ldg. Stokers Butler and Jenkins;
1st. Class Stokers Hancock, Harding, Plaskett, Finnegan and May;
Blacksmith O'Shea;
Armourer Frampton;
Painter 2nd Class Macey;
Ship's Cook Pattie;
Cpl. MacIntyre, RMLI;
Pvte. Adams and Faile, RMLI.

But, of course, it was the more modern vessels built by Palmers which took a more active part in the winning of the war at sea. As can be seen from the 'complete list of warships built' which follows, Palmers continued to receive orders throughout the war and, in 1915, were even called upon to 'turn the clock back' to their very first naval contract, when the Admiralty ordered three 'Monitors' (floating gun batteries) from the Jarrow shipbuilders.

These 'Monitors' were used to devastating effect

to shell the German coastal defences and trenches in Flanders. Indeed, throughout that momentous conflict, Palmers' vessels did credit to their builders, though not without cost, and many were lost in action.

One of Palmers' new "Monitors"; HMS "Marshall Ney" in action.

Therefore, it might have been expected that, when hostilities ended, Palmers would have received a fair share of the work assigned in the Naval rebuilding programme. It was not to be. Due to armaments reduction treaties, financial considerations and downright political favouritism, Palmers' claims were ignored and the great integrated complex was allowed to languish.

There were many bitter working men in Jarrow who said that, had Palmers been less patriotic and accommodating to the Admiralty, had they stuck to commercial and merchant ship construction, the famous old shipyard would have continued in business for many years longer.

As it was, the reward for their ingenuity and loyalty was redundancy.

On the 19th July, 1932, Palmers launched its verylast ship, *HMS Duchess*, a final commission for the Royal Navy.

Full List of all British Warships built by Palmers

(1856-1933)

Year	Type	Name or Number	Tonnage (Displacement)	Engine (h.p)
1856	Battleship*	Terror	1,844	200
1862	Battleship	Defence	6,270	2,540
1872	Battleship	Cerberus	3,480	1,670
1872	Battleship	Gorgon	3,480	1,670
1872	Battleship	Swiftsure	6,910	4,910
1872	Battleship	Triumph	6,910	4,910

** Descriptive terms, however, were notoriously loose in early years*

HMS 'Triumph', one of Palmers' first battleships.
Note that she still carried full sailing-ship rig.

HMS 'Dee', one of Palmers' Class of River Gunboats

Year	Type	Name or Number	Tonnage (Displacement)	Engine (h.p)
1875	River Gunboat	Medina	363	410
"	"	Medway	"	"
"	"	Sabrina	"	"
"	"	Spey	"	"
"	"	Slaney	"	"
1876	"	Esk	"	"
"	"	Tay	"	"
"	"	Tees	"	"
"	"	Don	"	"
"	"	Dee	"	"
"	"	Trent	"	"
"	"	Tweed	"	"

HMS 'Orlando', belted cruiser

Year	Type	Name or Number	Tonnage (Displacement)	Engine (h.p)
1879	Torpedo Miner	No 1	104	130
"	"	No 2	"	"
"	"	No 3	"	"
1880	Torpedo Miner	No 4	104	130
1881	"	No 5	"	"
"	"	No 8	"	"
"	"	No 9	"	"
"	"	No 10	"	"
1881	Torpedo Miner	No 13	104	130
"	"	No 14	"	"
1885	Cruiser	Surprise	1,650	3,000
"	"	Alacrity	"	"
1888	Cruiser	Orlando	5,000	8,500
"	"	Undaunted	"	"

HMS 'Resolution', first-class battleship

Year	Type	Name or Number	Tonnage (Displacement)	Engine (h.p)
1891	Cruiser	Pique	3,600	9,680
"	"	Rainbow	"	"
"	"	Retribution	"	"
1893	Battleship	Resolution	14,150	13,000
"	"	Revenge	"	"

HMS 'Bat', steaming at over 32 knots

Year	Type	Name or Number	Tonnage (Displacement)	Engine (h.p)
1895	Destroyer	Janus	252	3,790
"	"	Lightning	"	"
"	"	Porcupine	"	"
1897	Destroyer	Star	322	6,000
"	"	Whiting	"	"
"	"	Bat	"	"
"	"	Chamois	"	"
"	"	Crane	"	"
"	"	Flying Fish	"	"
1898	Destroyer	Fawn	"	"
"	"	Flirt	"	"

HMS 'Pyramus', she also served with distinction in World War One, but was luckier than her sister ship, the 'Pegasus'

Year	Type	Name or Number	Tonnage (Displacement)	Engine (h.p)
1898	Cruiser	Pegasus	2,135	7,000
"	"	Pyramus	"	"
1899	Destroyer	Spiteful	322	6,000
"	"	Peterel	"	"
1901	Destroyer	Myrmidon	322	6,000
"	"	Kangaroo	"	"
"	"	Syren	"	"
1902	Battleship	Russell	14,000	18,000
1904	Destroyer	Erne	560	7,000
"	"	Ettrick	"	"
"	"	Exe	"	"
"	"	Cherwell	"	"
"	"	Dee	"	"

HMS 'Sapphire'

Year	Type	Name or Number	Tonnage (Displacement)	Engine (h.p)
1905	Destroyer	Ure	560	7,000
"	"	Wear	"	"
"	"	Swale	"	"
"	"	Rother	"	"
1905	Cruiser	Sapphire	3,000	9,800
1908	Battleship	Lord Nelson	16,500	16,750
1909	1st Class Torpedo Boat	No.24	300	4,000
"	"	No.35	"	"
"	"	No.36	"	"
"	Destroyer	Albacore	440	8,000
"	"	Bonetta	"	"
1910	"	Viking	1,050	15,500

HMS 'Hercules'; she was the first R.N vessel to reach Kiel in order to receive the German surrender at the end of World War One

Year	Type	Name or Number	Tonnage (Displacement)	Engine (h.p)
1911	Battleship	Hercules	20,000	25,000
1913	Battle Cruiser	Queen Mary	27,000	75,000
1914	Destroyer	Leonidas	1,034	24,500
"	"	Lucifer	"	"
"	"	Murray	1,120	25,000
1915	"	Myngs	"	"
"	Monitor	General Wolfe	5,680	
"	"	Marshall Ney	6,770	
"	"	Marshall Soult	6,780	
1916	Battleship	Resolution	25,750	41,000
"	Submarine	E 39	810	
"	"	E 40	810	

Warships at Palmers' fitting-out berths on a misty morning

Year	Type	Name or Number	Tonnage (Displacement)	Engine (h.p)
1916	Destroyer	Nonsuch	1,120	25,000
"	"	Negro	"	"
"	"	Norman	"	"
"	"	Northesk	"	"
"	"	Oriole	"	"
"	"	Osiris	"	"
1917	Destroyer	North Star	"	"
"	"	Nugent	"	"
"	"	Urchin	"	27,000
"	"	Ursa	"	"
1918	"	Waterhen	1,420	"
"	"	Wryneck	"	"

HMS 'Stormcloud', one of the last R.N vessels to be built by Palmers

Year	Type	Name or Number	Tonnage (Displacement)	Engine (h.p)
1918	Cruiser	Dauntless	4,730	40,000
1919	Destroyer	Steadfast	1,120	27,000
"	"	Sterling	"	"
"	"	Stonehenge	"	"
1920	"	Stormcloud	"	"
1928	Cruiser	York	8,400	80,000
1930	Destroyer	Boreas	1,360	
1930	"	Brazen	1,360	
1932	"	Diana	1,375	
1932	"	Duchess	1,375	

"HMS Duchess", the last vessel built at Palmers' Yard, entering Tyne Dock.
Photo: Courtesy of "The Shields Gazette"

The First to Sink a 'Sub'!

The 'Thordis' alongside, on a more peaceful occasion

The distinction of being the first merchant vessel ever to sink a submarine was claimed by the Newcastle-registered steam collier *Thordis* which rammed and sank a German assailant on the 28th of February, 1915.

The *Thordis* had been peacefully proceeding, fully laden with 290 tons of Northumbrian coal, on a voyage from Blyth to Plymouth and was off Beachy Head when she was attacked by the submarine.

It was Sunday morning and the collier's master, Captain J.W Bell, was below when the second mate called him to the bridge to report that he had sighted a submarine on the starboard side.

German U-boat guncrew lining up to sink a helpless victim

By the time the master reached the bridge, however, the submarine had submerged so that only her periscope was visible. She then proceeded around the collier's stern, as Capt. Bell surmised, 'to take a look at us,, and this behaviour convinced him that she was an enemy vessel.

He therefore immediately ordered all hands on deck and the ship's boat to be put in readiness for launching. At this stage of the war, all-out and unrestricted submarine warfare had not yet been decreed by the German Admiralty and the crews of vessels were often allowed to lower their boats and to clear away before their ships were sunk by an attacking submarine.

Since the crew of a submarine was necessarily small, a 'prize crew' could not be spared and the submarine had little choice but to sink vessels captured in this way. The favoured method of sinking was to board and scuttle the captured vessel, since an expensive torpedo could not be spared for a battle already won. Alternatively, the victim might be sunk by gunfire, to give the gunners practice.

A dreaded sight; a U-boat orders a merchant vessel to heave-to, prior to sinking her

German submarines at this time were equipped with only four torpedoes, all fired from bow tubes, and it was necessary to return to base once these were expended. It is all the more surprising, therefore, that the German submarine's Captain decided to fire one of his precious torpedoes to dispose of a mere collier such as the *Thordis*. But, once the submarine had taken up position on his little ship's port beam, Capt Bell clearly saw a torpedo coming towards her.

Fortunately, or perhaps due to a lack of skill or experience on the part of her German assailant, the torpedo passed right under the collier, leaving her unscathed.

Acting with immediate and remarkable presence of mind, Capt Bell ordered the helm to be put hard over towards the submarine before she could line up and fire another torpedo. The collier had been proceeding at full speed at the time of the attack and, allowing for the tightness of her turn, it was at almost full speed that she ran over the enemy. The submarine's periscope was observed to be sheared off and, moments later, the little collier lurched with the force of the impact, all on board her hearing the distinct crunch of a collision.

Neither the submarine nor any of her crew were ever sighted again, but an oil slick rose to the surface of the water to mark her grave.

Further proof of the encounter was provided when the *Thordis* docked in Plymouth for repairs after discharging her cargo and it was found that she had sustained extensive damage to her keel plate and propeller.

Indeed, proof *was* required since various patriotic donors had offered a £1000 prize to the first merchant vessel to sink one of the enemy's submarines which, in the hysteria of war, were being represented in the press as 'pirates'.

Before Capt. Bell and his crew could claim their prize money, however, another vessel, the steamer *Alston*, owned by Messrs. Webster and Barraclough of West Hartlepool, lodged a prior claim. The *Alston*, according to a telegram sent by her master, Capt. Wyatt of Barrow, had rammed and sunk a submarine on the 27th of February, on the day *before* the exploit of the *Thordis*. Since the *Alston* was still at sea, proceeding on a voyage to the River Plate, the Admiralty ruled that the respective merits of the claims could not be settled until she had docked and full details of her claim had been investigated.

Though Capt. Bell was so anxious that his prize money would be snatched from him that he declared that he would not put to sea again until his claim was settled, he need not have been unduly worried. Such was the strength of public feeling on the subject of the enemy 'pirates', that there seemed to be no end to the inducements offered to those who dared to retaliate against them.

First, a Cardiff shipowner, Mr. Tatem, announced that he would award £500 to the *second* merchant

Admiral Von Pohl, Chief of German Marine Staff. He was forced to raise the stakes when the hunters became the hunted

vessel to sink an enemy submarine and then, not to be outdone, Joseph Hoult, chairman of Ben Line Steamers, offered £500 to each of the next *four* merchant vessels or trawlermen to "sink a sub".

In the event, the Admiralty finally ruled that Capt. Bell's claim was the stronger and not only awarded him the prize money, but also appointed him a Lieutenant of the Royal Naval Reserve and summoned him to London to be presented with the Distinguished Service Cross by the King. The Admiralty itself also granted a further £200 to be distributed amongst the crew of the *Thordis* and her owners gave Capt. Bell a gold watch.

The unfortunate effect of all this public-spirited generosity, however, was to infinitely 'raise the stakes' in submarine warfare. So many subsequent attempts were made to ram German submarines that often the 'hunters became the hunted' and many British merchant vessels began to actually *seek* encounters with the enemy in the hope of making their fortunes! Beside the obvious dangers of such an attitude, the effect on the position of the German Admiralty was catastrophic. Civilians who attacked the Kaiser's armed forces, whether on land or at sea, would be dealt with in the same way as traitors and spies, it was eventually announced.

On the 26th July, 1916, the British sea captain Charles Fryatt was condemned to death by a German naval court-martial and executed by firing squad, despite considerable public feeling in Germany that he ought to be pardoned. He had attempted to ram his ship *Brussels* into the German U-boat U33 when the latter had ordered him to stop.

Captain Charles Fryatt.
Executed by Firing-Squad

No matter how heroic his behaviour, the court-martial ruled that he had acted as a member of the British armed forces without wearing the uniform of his country. Masters of vessels like the *Thordis* would have to think twice now before they put their helm hard over!

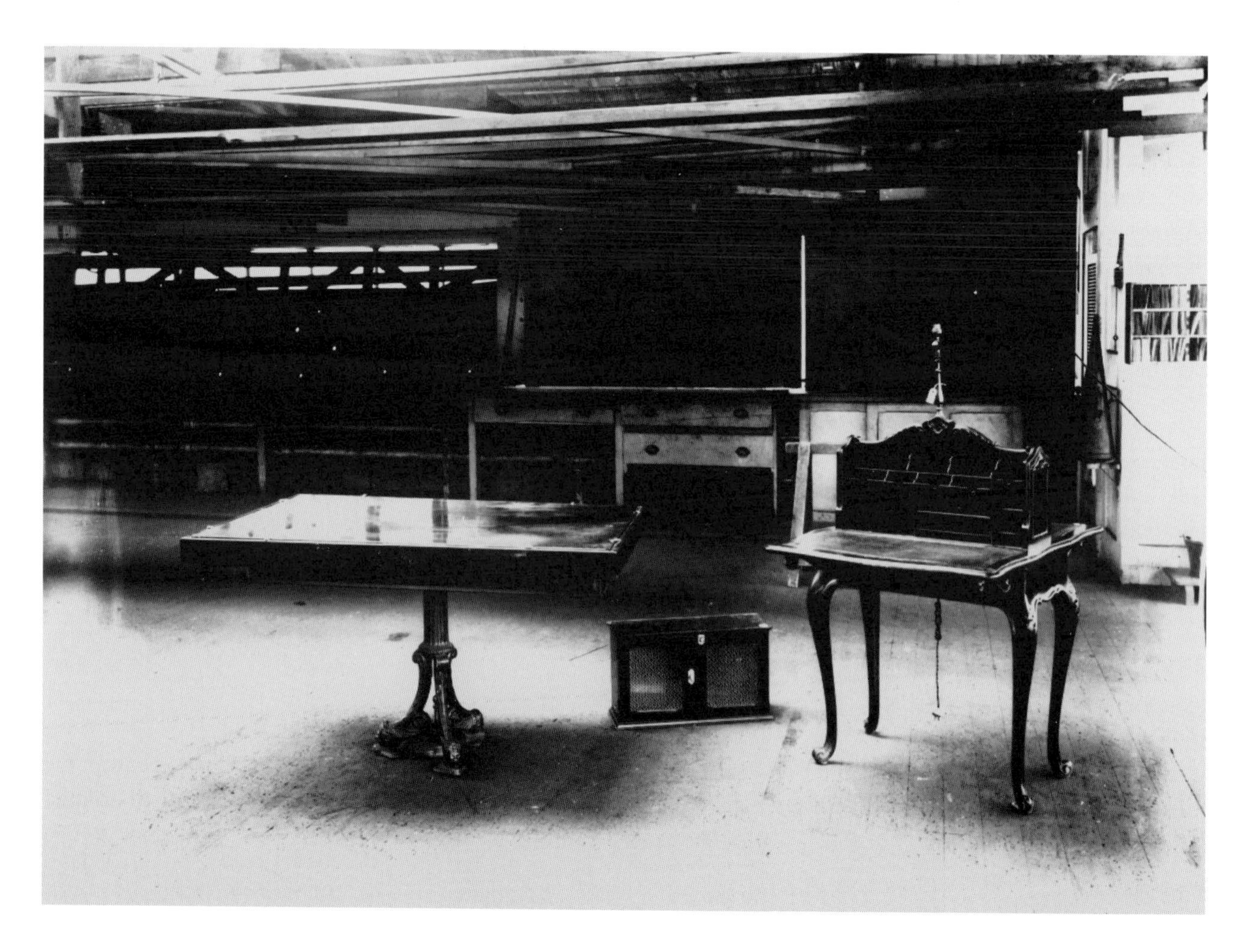

The "Olympic" auction. Luxurious fittings laid out for sale on the great liner's deck.
(photo courtesy of "The Shields Gazette")

The Death of the 'Olympic'

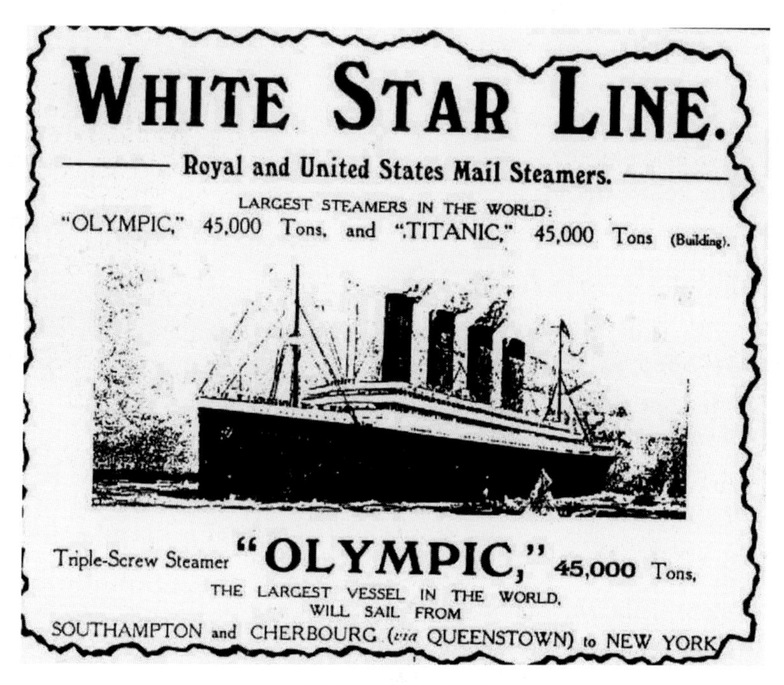

HAPPIER DAYS
A poster advertising the 'Olympic', at launch

In 1934, the famous old shipyard of Jarrow Palmers was bought by National Shipbuilders Security Ltd for dismantling.

A 'covenant' had been signed by the purchasers, promising that no ships would be built or repaired on the site for 40 years, so as to lessen the competition for other shipyards. No one seems to have given much thought to the workers and there was terrible hardship in the town.

Jarrow, of course, was not unique in this respect. There was terrible hardship everywhere in the 'hungry thirties', especially among those who made their living in the shipping industry. Even the rich were 'feeling the pinch', and luxury liner companies could no longer rely upon filling the first-class accommodation of their 'blue riband' ships for the prestigious Atlantic crossings.

In May, 1934, the Atlantic fleets of those two most

deadly rivals, The White Star Line and Cunard, were forced into amalgamation in order to survive. A severe 'rationalisation' of the combined fleet was inevitable, and this sounded the death-knell for many venerable and proud ships. One such was the *Olympic*, sister to the *Titanic,* which had been built at the same yard and had made her maiden voyage only months before her ill-fated and, consequently, more famous sister ship.

At 22 years of age, *Old Reliable*, as she was affectionately nicknamed, was finding it increasingly difficult to keep up with the demanding standards of the newer ships. Despite her proud nickname, the *Olympic* had experienced a rather chequered career and it was evident to all that she had made her last trip.

Dashing poster advertising the new ship, 1911

Launched on the 29th October, 1910, just seven months before her more famous sister, *The Titanic*, her career had been far from incident-free. During her first year of service, on the 20th September 1911, she had been severely damaged in a collision with the battlecruiser HMS *Hawke* in Southampton roads.

During that same year, the *Olympic* was involved in the first ever charter flight when W. A. Burpee, an American millionaire passenger, broke his spectacles before the ship departed from New York. The glasses were duly repaired and Thomas Sopwith, inventor of the famous Camel biplane, was hired to overtake the *Olympic* at sea and drop the well-cushioned package on to the liner's deck.

On the 27th October, 1914, the *Olympic* repaid her debt to the Royal Navy when she attempted to take the stricken battleship HMS *Audacious* in tow. The attempt failed and the battleship sank, but the *Olympic* rescued the entire crew.

In September 1915, the grand old lady's luxurious fittings were ripped out or boarded over and she was converted into a troopship for the duration of the First World War. It was during this time, when she made over twenty successful Atlantic crossings, that she earned the nickname *Old Reliable* from the soldiers she transported. It was also during this period that she showed her fighting qualities. During her 22nd troopship voyage, on the 12th of May 1918, she was attacked by U103. Avoiding the submarine's torpedo, the *Olympic* rammed and sank her assailant.

Returning to passenger service in July 1920, she was never far from the headlines, carrying the rich and famous, including Charlie Chaplin, back and forth across 'the pond'. In July 1929, she was sensationally shaken by an undersea earthquake whilst en-route to New York, but she weathered the storm without casualties.

On the 16th May 1934, she disgraced herself again when she rammed and sank the Nantucket Lightvessel in thick fog. Seven of the Lightship's crew were lost and the U.S Government demanded half-a-million dollars in compensation. It was soon after this incident, in March 1935, that she was withdrawn from passenger service.

On August 20th, 1935, whilst lying at Southampton, the *Olympic* was opened for inspection to prospective purchasers for scrapping or refit. A rumoured negotiation with the Italian government having broken down, it was announced on September 10th that she had been purchased by Sir John Jarvis, a London financier, to be scrapped.

Sir John Jarvis paid £100,000 for the vessel and immediately sold it on for the same price to Thomas W. Ward & Co. Ltd., of Sheffield, on condition that the work of dismantling be carried out at Palmers' Yard, Jarrow. Sir John did this in order to bring work into the town. As High Sheriff of Surrey, he had some time previously persuaded

The 'Olympic' emerges from the mist

the affluent folk of his county to 'adopt' the township of Jarrow. A fund had been set up and many schemes were launched by this energetic entrepreneur to alleviate the distress in the town and to help its workfolk back on to their feet. By bringing the *Olympic* to Jarrow, he hoped to initiate a major new industry, shipbreaking, on the site of the famous old shipyard. After all, the 'covenant', though banning shipbuilding and repair, said nothing about ship*breaking*. The death of the *Olympic* was to be a rebirth for Jarrow, or so Sir John earnestly hoped.

On Friday, October 11th, 1935, at 4.30pm, the *Old Reliable* set off from Southampton for Jarrow, on what was projected to be her last trip. Her arrival was awaited with eager anticipation on Tyneside.

Sir John Jarvis (pointing and wearing a bowler hat) watches the 'Olympic' arrive (photo courtesy of The Shields Gazette)

High tide was at 3.50pm on the day of her arrival, so the great ship was forced to lie off the Tyne for almost six hours before she could make her grand entrance to the river.Three miles off Herd Sands, she patrolled up and down in the morning haze as the crowds built up on shore, her pinky-beige funnels glinting in the autumn sunshine. Starved of a clear view of the famous old vessel, the crowds strained to glimpse her through the morning mist. The tension built up and public interest was even greater than had been anticipated.

That day's *Shields Gazette* reported that:

> "one of the largest crowds was on the Lawe Top, where the road was scarcely passable at times. Hundreds of people thronged the South Pier and the terraces of the South Marine Park and there was an especially large crowd on the Groyne Pier."

It was noticeable how much larger the crowds were for this than for other such sad occasions, such as the last trip of the *Mauritania*, which had returned to the Tyne for scrapping on July the 2nd of that same year. It was as though people finally knew that this really *was* the end of an era.

Even the rather rickety wooden Pilot Jetty was invaded by spectators determined to get a better view, many old seadogs clutching "ancient telescopes which had been unearthed for the occasion". In Jarrow, rather fittingly, the top of a ballast hill near the Merchantile Dock had been designated as the official vantage point for the

The 'Olympic' arrives in the Tyne
(Photo courtesy of The Shields Gazette)

party of civic dignitaries and industrial leaders who were gathering to welcome the great ship to her last resting place.

At five minutes to three, the *Olympic* resolutely turned her nose westward and, under her own steam, headed for the Tyne. Once she was abreast The Narrows, however, the welcoming party of six tugs, like undertaker's assistants, closed in.

> "As if firmly resolved not to stand any nonsense, the *Hendon* and the *Joffre* moved under her bows, each taking a thick hawser aboard her, while the *Wearmouth* jostled fiercely against the *Olympic's* starboard flank, so that the hemp buffers groaned in protest. Meanwhile, the tugs *Plover* and *George V* had taken hold at the stern."

She was like a great stag, beset by hounds. The sixth tug, *Great Emperor*, cruised nearby, as though watchful that there should be no escape.

In what seemed like shocked silence, the huge crowds watched. As she glided through the piers,

The 'Olympic' passing South Shields Ferry Landing
(Photo courtesy of The Shields Gazette)

it could be seen that, instead of the diplomats, international financiers, millionaires and film stars who had strolled her decks in the past, only a hundred honest British seamen lined her rails, staring dumbly at the crowds.

Overhead, a plane dipped and wheeled in salute and, circling like a vulture, the T.E.C ferryboat, placed at the disposal of the press, recorded her progress from every angle, newsreel cameras whirring. Slowly, silently, with quiet dignity, the great ship slid on by.

"And then the liner spoke. A rusty old trawler, caked with North Sea salt, started her off. From the Fish Quay moorings she screamed and shrieked on her whistle as if for dear life and it was the signal for every craft for miles around to join in the chorus of welcome.

"The sound died and the silence fell. Heralded by a gushing plume of white steam from her

The 'Olympic arrives at Jarrow
(Photo courtesy of The Shields Gazette)

forward funnel came the *Olympic's* reply — three long blasts in a deep and tremulous bass — so low as to be just audible to human ears and full of sadness and melancholy."

And all along the river, the cheering began.

On both banks of the Tyne, the people roared their proud response. Those who had built the ships and those who had sailed in them, those who had dug the coal and those who had smelted the steel, they were all there that day to make their presence felt. There was to be nothing pathetic about the *Olympic's* progress up the Tyne, the people of Tyneside saw to that.

"By this time the river was choc-a-bloc with craft of every description. Shabby little motor-boats stuttering on one cylinder rubbed the paint off dapper pleasure launches whose occupants had paid a shilling to see the sights. The *Olympic* was preceded by the Harbour Master's launch, while police patrol boats saw to it that intrepid oarsmen were not rammed by the liner's stem.

"Past Whitehill Point, past Tyne Dock, the

convoy slid at a steady two knots. Every now and then, at some particularly tricky bend in the river, a whistle would blow from the *Olympic's* bridge with shrill urgency and in response some of the tugs would nose against the iron of the ship, their engines spinning yet more savagely, until the water behind them was churned into foam."

And still the cheers rang out. Those who had reckoned to follow the progress of the great ship by walking along the riverbank were thwarted both by the unexpected speed of the convoy's progress and the immovable density of the roaring crowds.

"Three quarters of an hour after crossing the river bar, the *Olympic* was abreast of the berth which had been prepared for her at Palmers' Yard, Jarrow. Warping the vessel in took another forty minutes and, in the opinion of expert observers, provided the most spectacular display of seamanship the Tyne has witnessed for years."

"Gently, with infinite slowness, the *Olympic*'s stem was brought nearer the quay. Scarcely a ripple disturbed the surface of the water as the tugs hauled her in, inch by inch. When the cutwater was a mere twenty feet from the bank, the *Hendon* drew in her hawser and slid away to reinforce the pushing movement which was being carried out by two other tugs on the starboard quarter. Slowly and inexorably, the *Olympic* was driven in towards the wharf."

The men of the Tyne had shown, once again, how well they could handle ships, even at the death.

The engines were shut down for the last time and the boiler fires allowed to go out. It must have been heartbreaking for the engineers who, to the end, had kept the machinery gleaming and immaculate. In the local press, Chief Engineer McKimm, who for 24 years had served aboard the great vessel, railed bitterly against her destroyers. Now all was to be stripped and sold off.

Visitors admiring the fine carved woodwork, whilst an arrow points out the permitted route (Photo courtesy of The Shields Gazette)

The auctioneer's men were already aboard, sizing up the lots. The auction was to commence within a month and there was much to be done, preparing the equipment and fittings for the bidders, who were expected to come from far afield, even from Europe and America.

But first, even while these preparations were taking place, the public were to be allowed to pay their last respects. For a fee of one shilling, the great ship was to be thrown open to visitors, so that, for once in their lives, the humble folk who built the liners could see for themselves 'how the other half lived', and share in the luxury at last.

Correctly discerning the level of public interest, the *Shields Gazette* generously gave away 100 free tickets to their readers, and printed the following list of lucky winners in their edition of Friday, 18/10/35;

These lucky youngsters look hardly typical of the Jarrow public (Photo courtesy of The Shields Gazette)

Mrs Pinnock, 62 Ferry St
Alec A Scott, 8 Williams St
S Hudson, 51 Clayton St
Mrs J Knowles, 53 Wear St
Mrs J Byres, 35 York St
D Wright, 9 Back Hibernian Rd
Thos Walls, 8 Ormonde St
Miss N Leonard, 45 Princess St
Walter Gill, 89 Clayton St
H Brown, 3 Derby St
Rbt Smith, 38 Station St
Mr Heanac, 37a Shelton St
Mrs J Patterson, 21 Field Terr.
Mr R Dawson, 42 Newmack St
Mrs J Drydon, 104a York St

Mrs Bennell, 38 Sheldon St
Mrs Fielding, 32 Berkeley St
Miss E Adams, 5 Hibernian Rd
Mrs Turnbull 39 Potter St
V Hope 28a Hope St
Agnes Sadler, 77 Buddle St
E Russell, 89 James St
Mrs H Morgan, 3 Wylam St
A McBride, 7 Cobden St
William Charman, 19 Edith St
A Collins, 15 Charles St
Mrs F Rowland, 14 Hylton Rd
F Southern, 73 Monkton Rd
Mrs Lily Dobson, 3 Wood Terr
E Mason, 12 Cuthbert St

Mrs A Ritchie, 25 Oak St
Mrs Chisholm, 194 High St
Mrs A Chatt, 10 Don St
Mr C Connelly, 36 Princess St
James Connor, 60 Queens Rd
F Hunter, 17 Clyde St
A Forster, 8 Maple St
Mrs Humphries, 54 Walter St
Madge Richardson, 6 Wylam St
Mrs Wright, 162 St Paul's Rd
Mrs W Chambers, 25 Palmer St
M Laidlaw, 110 York St
Mrs Carr, 20 Wilberforce St
Mrs R Watt, 69 James St
Mrs Gill 43 Howard St

Mrs Taylor, 18 Simonside View
Mr S Roberts, 13 Hylton Rd
Mrs Miller, 12 Connaught Terr.
Rbt E Spoor, 30 Queen's Rd
J A Lesner, 10 Biscop Terr.
James Burns, 60 Albert Rd
Mr G Pearson, 3 Penshaw View
John Smith, 39 Chaytor St
M Coatsworth, 10 Tweed St
Mr R S Smith, 4 Tweed St
Hilda Batey, 32 Primrose Terr.
Miss Paxton, 21 Salem St
Mr S Hogg, 7 Richards St
E Adams, 21 Bede Burn Rd
J Maugham, 64 James St
Mrs Weatherson, 33 Clyde St
G W Swift, 12 South St
Betty Leonard, 91 McIntyre St
David Kyle, 57 Monkton Terr.
Rose Downey, 86 McIntyre St
M Barrett, 47 Union St
Miss Bryce, 15 Russell St
R Beattie, 35 High St
L Richards, 96 Dee St
R Suddick, 68 Grange Rd West
Mrs Cole, 50 Hibernian Rd
Mrs Sayers, 15 Hibernian Rd
Mrs Hughes, 173 Albert Rd
Mrs I Usher, 49 Clayton St
Mrs Batty, 14 Clayton St
C Newstead, 12 Hill St
May Baker, 23 Nansen St
Miss M Wilson, Chaytor St

Ward employees at the gangway.
They were granted a special tour.
(Photo courtesy of The Shields Gazette)

S Thynn, 12 Wear St
Mary Maghan, 33 St Paul's Rd
Mrs K Crawford, 6 Grange Rd
Thomas Gallant, 9 Leopold St
Mrs T Mongan, 115 Ellison St
Winifred Todd, 22 Roman Rd
Mrs Collings, 17 Charles St
Mrs H I Smith, 42 Clayton St
A S Gault, 40 Shakespeare St
Mrs Hipkin, 9 Short Row
Mrs Morreno, 34 Duke St
M Coulthard, 1 North View
Mrs Elliot, 99 Clayton St

Mrs M Trotter, 33 Stanley St
Mr Keeble, 22 Clyde St
Henry Mallen, 60 Clayton St
S Ronaldson, 92 James St
Mrs C Matthews, 55 Russell St
Mrs Alice Dodds, 8 Bridge St
Mrs Campbell, 42 Stead St
M A Leonard, 102 Ellison St

and Henry L Bland of 21 Nixon Street, the house in which the author of this book was born,. ten years later.

The ship actually stood open to visitors for ten days until Saturday 26th October and, despite the relatively high price of admission (a shilling was enough to supply a good meal for a hungry family amongst the masses of Jarrow's unemployed), many thousands filed aboard to be shepherded around in mute admiration, wandering through those of the palatial staterooms which as yet remained unplundered.

No better description of the event could be written than that which appeared in the *Shields Gazette*;

> "Flags and bunting, grimy but bravely indicative of new hopes at Jarrow, flutter lazily between the houses in Ellison Street, the main approach to the shipbreaking yard where the towering bulk of the *Olympic* lies.
>
> "At the top of the street, buses unload passengers, sightseers anxious to spend a shilling to wander through vast and ornate rooms which millionaires have trod and which are now merely dismal show places. For ten days, the solitary turnstile at the entrance to Palmers' Yard has clicked as thousands of people began their trudge through the almost deserted yard.
>
> "Stocks, once massive with the bulk of great ships, tower gaunt towards the sky. Rusty rails no longer carry fussy locomotives. Ahead lies the *Olympic*, veteran of one and a half million ocean miles, slightly rusty but magnificently impressive in its bulk.
>
> "Crowds file up the gangway - people who are used to ships, others making their first acquaintance with an ocean liner. Disappointment awaits those who expect an unrestricted saunter along spacious decks and through low-ceilinged rooms. Ropes and chains bar the way and hurriedly chalked arrows silently indicate the permitted route to the wanderer. Dim lights in a few staterooms show the magnificence which once was, others are already stripped and forbidding. Only a few bright spots of light illuminate the drawing room and smoking room.
>
> "People follow each other in long lines trying to visualise the scene when the *Olympic* was a complete ship, complete with its passengers and sumptuous in its fine furnishings.
>
> "The long file moves on through the mortuary to the infectious hospital and then stops as people crush by the huge quadrant of the ship's steering gear to the kitchens, where only a few pans have been left. Feet shuffle on linoleum, for the carpets have gone, as have so many other things on the *Olympic*.
>
> "Today the stream of sightseers which has passed down Ellison Street almost continuously for the last ten days will stop. Then there will be a breathing space on board the former largest British-built passenger ship until November 5th, when auctioneers and dealers will foregather to continue the dismembering of the mighty ship. Even now the lot numbers are on many pieces of panelling and on fine articles of furniture. Eventually, the last lot will go under the hammer and the *Olympic* will have seen the last of her rich patrons.
>
> "A fine ship, now useless for the purpose for which she was built will have vanished, but parts of her will remain. One day a firescreen, for instance, may grace some suburban home. It may be a part of a ship which once rammed an enemy submarine."

At the conclusion of the public viewing days, although for some reason accurate figures were not available, the *Gazette* thought that "several tens of thousands" of visitors had paid their shilling to trudge round the areas so grudgingly left open to them. Indeed, a pattern of stinginess was beginning to develop in Jarrow's dealings with the ship-breakers, a pattern which was eventually to frustrate Sir John Jarvis' good intentions.

Meanwhile, the auctioneers, Messrs Knight, Frank & Rutley of London, complained that "small articles which have disappeared from some of the cabins indicate that among the visitors have been enthusiastic but none too scrupulous souvenir hunters".

It appeared that at least a few of the ordinary working folk of Jarrow made sure that they got something more than a quick look for their shilling!

During the days before the auction began, excitement mounted, not least among the officials of Messrs Knight, Frank & Rutley, who were anticipating a bumper sale.

Ornate Fanlight from the 'Olympic', now in the White Swan Hotel, Alnwick.

Why, even a souvenir stall which had been set up at the foot of the gangway during the public visits had made a roaring trade and, the auctioneers gleefully reported, "some visitors willingly paid quite substantial prices for such small articles as (clothes) hangers." Doubtless this went some way towards compensating the vendors for the articles which had been 'liberated' by other, less honest or affluent, visitors.

30,000 identification tickets had been attached to the items to be sold and some 4,456 lots were featured in the sumptuous catalogue. This publication, a gorgeous quarto-sized affair of 365 pages, retailed at two shillings and sixpence and, as that was about twice their hourly rate (see 'final word'), it is not likely that many were sold to the men who worked on the great vessel's demolition.

The delighted auctioneers further reported that "British and foreign art dealers and souvenir hunters were expected to visit Jarrow in their hundreds" for the sale and that "keen bidding" was "promised from a small group of American dealers" who were thought to be interested in the furnishings of the "state rooms in which they have in past years crossed the Atlantic". Even the general public were expected to make "a sentimental rush" for "small items of the liner's fittings" to be offered at the sale.

Unsurprisingly, given the level of anticipation, the event proved a disappointment to the auctioneers, who later grumbled that they could have raised more from the sale if they had held it in Southampton after all. It appeared that, in spite of the influx of foreign buyers, there just wasn't enough money around on Tyneside to "bid the items up".

Nevertheless, the sale started with high hopes. Mr Arthur Knight himself made a moving little speech before offering the first lot and no one had any doubts as to his sincerity. Not many auctions can have been started with such an elegant tribute as this;

> "I have, in my time, broken up many a noble and historic home; and today I have the unhappy task of performing the last rites for this magnificent ship which has been for many years the home of the gallant crews sailing in her. It is impossible to be unmoved by helping to destroy such a monument to man's achievement, and I feel I owe the *Olympic* my apologies before starting my undignified labours."

The first lot was then offered, a pair of settees from the engineers' smokeroom, which was knocked down for £7. Other lots followed in quick succession but, in general, no real 'bidding-wars' developed and the expected inflation of prices did not occur.

Among the lots which *did* raise substantial sums was the furniture of the staterooms which had once been occupied by the Prince of Wales, later to be King Edward VIII. The first of these, in ormolu-mounted mahogany, realised £87. The second suite, in carved satinwood, was sold for £42, both lots being bought by Mr. H. Hutton, of the Marquis of Granby Hotel, Bamford, near Sheffield. The biggest buyer, of 394 lots in all, was Mr C. T. Hawtree, of the Majestic Lido Hotel, Douglas, Isle of Man.

During the second week of the sale, however, interest waned to such an extent that, at the end, several lots were left with the auctioneers. Three of the electric lifts from the first-class passenger accommodation went for £30 each, a great bargain in anybody's money.

Local buyers included Messrs. J. Hogg & Sons,

Fine panelling from the 'Olympic' to be seen today at The White Swan Hotel, Alnwick.

of North Shields, who bought the ship's bell for 26 guineas, whilst the White Swan Hotel of Alnwick and Hadrian Paints Ltd, of Haltwhistle, bought panelling from the first-class accommodation which is still in use today.

At the very time that the proud ship was being dismembered, a tragic coincidence occurred. One of her most famous commanders, Captain Walter Henry Parker, CBE, RNR, died at his home in Surrey.

Captain Parker, a seadog of the 'old school', had served his time in sailing ships and gained his first command at the age of only 24. He was a war hero, having commanded convoys, and had had charge of no less than 261 ships, laden with troops and ammunition, during those momentous years.

Whilst in command of the *Olympic,* he had met many film stars, financial magnates and millionaires, experiences which he had described in his memoirs, 'Leaves from an Unwritten Logbook', published in 1931.

And now, at the age of only 66, he died with his ship.

This complete staircase, which once graced the ship, now leads to the 'Olympic Lounge' at the White Swan Hotel, Alnwick.

Epilogue

Sir John Jarvis' philanthropic hope of establishing a major shipbreaking industry at Palmers' Yard did not materialise. After removing all the equipment of the yard itself, Thomas W. Ward Ltd. did not even complete the dismantling of the *Olympic* at Jarrow.

After two years, in which everything of value was stripped from her, her bare hulk was towed back down the Tyne, en route for Inverkeithing in Scotland, where she was finally cut to pieces.

On the 19th September, 1937, the carcass of the great ship, which had arrived in such glory, was towed silently downriver, in the charge of a posse of tugs.

During the previous autumn, the town had staged its last protest. 200 of its fittest former workers had marched to London to hand in a petition asking for work. The situation was beyond the powers of individuals, good men such as Sir John Jarvis. The people of the town asked for Government intervention.

They asked in vain. Only the intervention of Adolf Hitler brought shipyard work back to Palmers of Jarrow.

The saddest sight of all; the hulk of the 'Olympic' leaves the Tyne (Photo courtesy of The Shields Gazette)

The Final Word

In 1991, Mr Alan Turner, a former shipyard worker, wrote a letter to *The Evening Chronicle*, some extracts of which, with his permission, I reproduce below;

"It occurred to me that I might well be one of the few persons remaining who were employed in the demolition of the ship which was built alongside the *Titanic* by Harland and Wolff of Belfast.

"I saw her come into Jarrow in 1935 under her own steam and soon after I secured employment aboard her, at age 16, for 17/6d (87p) per 48 hour week.

"Working with a joiner, who was an ex-foreman in the old Jarrow Palmers Shipyard, I helped to strip off the panelling from a stateroom. This panelling can now be seen in the White Swan Hotel, in Alnwick.

"I also helped dismantle the ornamental glass dome from the ceiling about the staircase on A Deck which is now, with some panelling, in Haltwhistle, in the old Hadrian paintworks. I lifted the floor tiles from the swimming pool and often see them in a front garden here in Hebburn.

"The *Olympic* was secured by Sir John Jarvis and the people of Surrey to be sent to Palmers' Jarrow yard to create employment in the depression of the 30's.

"Thomas W. Ward of Sheffield did the demolition and employed men with a wage little more than the dole. Two pounds two shillings (£2.10p) was paid for a 48-hour week to everyone over 21.

"Acetylene burners were paid extra for medicine because of the fumes from the paint when they were cutting up the platework. Later they were given two square packets of Epsom Salts costing 1/2d each (6p) and their other medicine allowance was stopped.

"The Jarrow Crusade, when the march to London took place in October, 1936, revealed the struggle people experienced just to keep alive.

"At that time, five men working on the *Olympic*, acting as spokesmen for their mates, went to the management and asked for a halfpence an hour rise (there was no trade union backing). The five men were dismissed for their temerity, no one backed them up and they received no unemployment benefit.

"In 1939, I worked on the *Berengaria* for a while and the conditions weren't improved when she was demolished. While they were at it, Thomas W. Ward broke up the whole shipyard.

"I do not look back on those days with any nostalgia."

Selected Bibliography

The Keelmen
Eric Forster, pub. Frank Graham, 1970.

Allan's Tyneside Songs
Thomas Allan, pub. Frank Graham, 1972.

The Tyne and its Tributaries
W. J. Palmer, pub Bell & Sons, 1882.

The Making of the River Tyne
R. W. Johnson, pub. Walter Scott, 1895.

John Bowes and the Bowes Museum
C. E. Hardy, pub. Frank Graham.

The Steam Collier Fleets
Macrae and Waine, pub. Waine Research.

Palmers' Yard and the Town of Jarrow
V. Rea, pub. Jarrow, 1975.

The Dictionary of Business Biographies (Vol 4)
Ed. D. J. Jeremy, pub. Butterworth, London.

Men of Mark Twixt Tyne and Tweed
Richard Welford, pub. Walter Scott, Newcastle 1895.

The River Tyne
James Guthrie, pub. Reid, 1880.

Garibaldi's Defence of the Roman Republic
G. M. Trevelyan, pub. Longmans, 1907.

Garibaldi and the Thousand
G. M. Trevelyan, pub. Penguin Books, 1965.

Garibaldi and the Making of Italy
G. M. Trevelyan, pub. Longmans, 1948.

Garibaldi and his Enemies
Christopher Hibbert, pub. Longmans, 1965.

Europe since 1815
C.D Hazen, pub. G. Bell & Son, 1909.

The Rhymes of the Northern Bards
Bell, 1812.

The Northern Minstrel
Marshall,1806-7.

The Newcastle Songster
Marshall, 1816.

Sketches of Coal Mines of Northumberland and Durham
T. H. Hair.

Victorian Britain (the North-East)
Frank Atkinson, 1989.

A History of the Northern Music Hall
G. J. Mellor, 1970.

The North East Engineers Strikes of 1871
Allen, Clarke, McCord and Rowe, pub. Frank Graham, 1971.

The History of the United Society of Boilermakers and Iron and Steel Shipbuilders
D. C. Cummins, 1905.

The History of the Boilermakers' Society (Vol 1)
J. E. Mortimer, pub. Allen & Unwin, 1973.

Some Account of Palmers, 4th Edition
Private Pub.1909.

From Collier to Battleships
John F. Davison, Durham County Press Ltd, 1946.

The Private War of Seaman Stumpf
Ed. D. Horn, pub. Frewin, London, 1969.

Also contemporary copies of the following newspapers and periodicals;

The Newcastle Courant, The Newcastle Weekly Chronicle, The Shields Gazette, The Newcastle Mercury, The Sunderland Herald, The Jarrow Chronicle, The Monthly Chronicle, The North of England Advertiser, The Newcastle Garland, The Tyne Mercury, The London Illustrated News, The Newcastle Advertiser, The Newcastle Evening Chronicle, Richardson's Table Book, The North and South Shields Gazette.